GOOD TAXES

THE CASE FOR TAXING
FOREIGN CURRENCY EXCHANGE
AND OTHER FINANCIAL TRANSACTIONS

To Mario Bunge and Nicholas Rescher, who combined science and philosophy with extraordinary breadth and rigour, and showed me how good scholarship could be used to improve the quality of life.

GOOD TAXES

THE CASE FOR TAXING
FOREIGN CURRENCY EXCHANGE AND
OTHER FINANCIAL TRANSACTIONS

ALEX C. MICHALOS

SCIENCE FOR PEACE

Dundurn Press
Toronto • Oxford

Editor: Derek Paul
Designer: Sebastian Vasile
Printer: Webcom

Canadian Cataloguing in Publication Data

Michalos, Alex C.
    Good taxes: the case for taxing foreign currency exchange and other financial
    transactions

Co-published by Science for Peace.
Includes bibliographical references.
ISBN 0-88866-954-2

1. Foreign exchange – Taxation – North America.   I. Science for Peace (Association)
II. Title.

HG3902. M52 1997   336.2'7833245'097   C97-930122-x

1   2   3   4   5   BJ   01   00   99   98   97

The publisher wishes to acknowledge the generous assistance of the **Canada Council,** the **Book Publishing Industry Development Program** of the **Department of Canadian Heritage,** and the **Ontario Arts Council.**

Dundurn Press
2181 Queen Street East
Suite 301
Toronto, Ontario, Canada
M4E 1E5

Dundurn Press
73 Lime Walk
Headington, Oxford
England
OX3 7AD

Dundurn Press
250 Sonwil Drive
Buffalo, NY
U.S.A. 14225

CONTENTS

Preface

Books submitted for publication in our Dundurn series are accepted on their merits, compatibility with the purposes of Science for Peace, and timeliness of subject matter. Generally, a typescript is submitted to a process of peer review prior to acceptance. Authors wishing to publish through Science for Peace should write in the first instance to the Publications Committee, Science for Peace, H2, University College, Toronto, M5S 1A1.

We gratefully acknowledge the support of the Walter and Duncan Gordon Foundation for books in our Dundurn series.

Derek Paul,
Shirley Farlinger
Publications Committee

Acknowledgements

everal drafts of parts of this essay were presented at different places and several people have given me helpful criticism and encouragement. Presentations were made at the Third Annual International Conference Promoting Business Ethics, at Niagara University, New York (October 31-November 2, 1996), the World Conference on Quality of Life in Prince George, BC (August 22-25, 1996), the First World Congress of Business, Economics and Ethics in Tokyo, Japan (July 25-28, 1996), and the annual meeting of the BC Political Science Association in Prince George (May 4, 1996). I would like to thank Professor David Felix for kindly providing me with helpful advice as well as copies of his most recent work prior to its publication. Thanks are also due to Professor James Tobin, Jordan Grant, Peter Kenen, John Dillon, Toni Fletcher and Jean Smith for bringing other material to my attention, and to Ian Birch, Isabelle Grunberg and Howard Sobel for their helpful comments. I am especially grateful to Derek Paul and Shirley Farlinger for their careful reading and many suggestions for improving the original manuscript. Joanne Matthews' library and online research has provided a mine of good information and, thanks to Stan Beeler, large chunks of my document were recovered from the bowels of a computer system from Hell. Obviously none of these people should be blamed for any of my mistakes.

Introduction

enerally speaking, the aim of this book is to make the case for an international tax on foreign currency exchange transactions (a Tobin tax) and for an intranational financial transactions tax in Canada and the United States. Following some theoretical and historical observations on the relationships among public services, public debt and taxes, most of the book contains a kind of cost-benefit analysis of the proposition that, all things considered, the nations of the world ought (prudentially and morally) to initiate a Tobin tax and Canada and the United States in particular ought to initiate a broad-based financial transactions (securities transactions excise) tax. As a Canadian citizen, I have a greater stake in the situation in Canada than in the United States, but for most of the relevant issues to be discussed here, our national borders do not have much significance. In fact, as the book will demonstrate, there has been much more discussion of the issues by Americans than by Canadians.

Foreign currency exchange transactions are a species of financial transactions. More precisely, they are financial transactions in which by means of some sort of financial instrument (coins, currency, securities, etc.) the value of the asset in the currency of one country is exchanged for the value of the asset in the currency of some other country. Today there are no taxes on foreign currency exchange transactions, but the Nobel Laureate, James Tobin, recommended their introduction in 1972. Besides such international financial transactions across national boundaries, there are intranational financial transactions within national boundaries. There are also many countries with excise taxes on intranational financial transactions; e.g., taxes on the sale and/or purchase of stocks and/or bonds within a country. These include Argentina, Australia, Austria, Belgium, Brazil, Chile, China, Colombia, Denmark, Finland, France, Hong Kong, India, Italy, Japan, Malaysia, New Zealand, Portugal, Singapore, South Korea, Spain, Sweden, Switzerland, Taiwan, Thailand, and the United Kingdom (Spahn 1995, pp.51-54). Some other countries have had such taxes and phased them out (e.g., Germany and the United States). On the pages cited, Spahn listed the most salient features of the various taxes. For example, here is Spahn's entry for Switzerland.

Introduction

> There is a stamp duty levied on the transfer for valuable consideration of securities by a dealer in securities. The rate applies to the purchase price, and it is 0.15 percent for Swiss securities, and 0.3 percent for foreign securities. Securities include bonds, annuity bonds, mortgage bonds, treasury and bank notes, shares, profit-sharing certificates of investment funds, and commercial papers. Certain types of transactions are exempt from the duty (p.54).

What was novel about Tobin's tax was its focus on international transactions. What is complicated about this whole area of research, among other things, is the fact that a tax on such transactions inevitably raises questions about "foreign currency exchange equivalents" and exactly what sorts of financial instruments and assets are to be covered by the tax. The pursuit of satisfactory answers to these questions draws one into discussions of a wide variety of financial or securities transactions excise taxes. Studies of the advantages and disadvantages of financial transactions excise taxes typically have direct implications for Tobin taxes, and vice versa. The fact is, as Powers (1993, p.16) remarked, "All markets are linked. One really cannot do a thorough job of analysis in one market without studying what is happening in related markets. Hence, if you really want to understand the bond market, you need to analyze commodity markets, stock markets, currency markets, and interest rate markets. And if you really want to understand stock markets, you have to analyze bond markets, currency markets, and commodity markets, etc."

For countries such as Canada and the United States, which currently have no financial transactions excise taxes, the idea of introducing a Tobin tax may seem very whimsical indeed. Nevertheless, from the point of view of most other industrialized countries which have some form of financial transactions excise taxes, the idea of a Tobin tax is considerably less whimsical. According to Frankel (1996, p.56), "Those countries that have already tried securities transactions taxes—levied on trading in stocks and bonds, not foreign exchange transactions—have been motivated primarily by a desire to scoop up what is popularly seen as excessive compensation accruing to financial traders". Whatever apparent whimsy there is in the idea of introducing a Tobin tax in Canada and the United States, there really are some live options here which finally require political will more than anything else to bring them to fruition.

Granted that a Tobin tax would be maximally beneficial only if it were levied fairly comprehensively in all countries, covering all kinds of financial instruments, assets and institutions, I do not think that it merits the kind of offhand dismissal that it has been given by our federal

Finance Minister or the Governor of the Bank of Canada. According to news reports, the federal Minister of Finance, the Hon. Paul Martin, believes such a tax would be "unenforceable" and the Governor of the Bank of Canada, Gordon Thiessen, believes it would be "counter-productive" (Beauchesne 1995, p.C8). However, I will do my best to convince you that a Tobin tax is not only feasible but very desirable, and that progressive people everywhere should be appealing to their governments to press for the development of such taxes at home and in appropriate international organizations such as the United Nations. Obviously insofar as my case for a Tobin tax is persuasive, the case for the introduction of a more modest intranational financial transactions excise tax in Canada and the United States should be even more persuasive. There is such a variety of these sorts of taxes in so many countries that it is simply beyond reasonable belief that nothing of the sort can succeed in North America. Indeed, by the end of my book, it should be clear that the main thing preventing us from introducing such a tax in Canada is the fact that we have not yet elected a federal government with the political will to do it.

The Politics of Debt, Taxes and Services

In this section I provide a brief sketch of some of the history of the Canadian federal government's accumulated debt in order to show again that there is overwhelming evidence that the debt is primarily the result of government policies and actions designed to decrease tax revenues and to increase real interest rates (pursuing a zero inflation rate), rather than the result of excessive spending on social programs. Excellent and much more detailed accounts may be found in McQuaig (1995), Workman (1996) and Klein (1996). Readers interested in a similar account for the United States may consult Greider (1987) and Block (1996). It is necessary to continue repeating this true story because most of Canada's political leaders and the popular press continue to repeat the false story that excessive spending has driven governments into such deep holes that they can no longer afford further social spending on anything like a reasonable social safety net or, to use a more traditional phrase, on a reasonable welfare state.

In fact, the size of the social safety nets in the relatively wealthy OECD (Organization for Economic Cooperation and Development) countries such as Canada has, at least since the 1950s, been mainly a matter of politics rather than economics (McQuaig 1993). Poverty statistics regarding lone parent families may be used to illustrate my point. In 1987, 45% of lone parent families with children under age 18 in Canada were classified as low income families and 53% of such lone parent families were classified that way in the United States in 1986, while only 6% were classified that way in Sweden and 8% in the Netherlands in 1987 (Smeeding and Rainwater 1991, p.67). Although Sweden and the Netherlands were certainly not six or eight times as wealthy as Canada and the United States, the former countries apparently cared more than the latter countries about the elimination of poverty through state welfare programs. (The 1991 public debt as a percent of GDP in Sweden was 46%, compared to 78% in Canada; United Nations Development Program 1994, p.198.) While I do not imagine that everything that is possible in Sweden and the Netherlands is possible (or even desirable) in Canada and the United

States, I do think that with appropriate education, political action and taxation, governments could do much more to improve the quality of people's lives at much lower costs, all things considered.

Based on his analysis of data for the 23 countries of the OECD in the 1965-1983 period, David R. Cameron (1985, p.260) produced the best short explanation I have ever seen of the politics underlying the relationships between the provision of public services, the creation of debt and the levying of taxes. This is it.

> Evidently, enduring control of government by leftist parties allows nations to enjoy the benefits of a large and expanding public economy — for example, relatively generous provision of social security benefits, social assistance, and unemployment compensation — while avoiding whatever macroeconomic costs are produced by large deficits! How? By imposing relatively high taxes—especially taxes on personal incomes and wealth. In contrast, nations in which non-leftist parties usually govern are more likely to experience a smaller, more miserly public economy (especially when conservatives dominate government) and a chronic 'fiscal crisis' reflected in relatively large deficits (especially when centrist and Christian Democratic parties dominate government). Why? Again, in large part because such parties—in particular, those which are conservative—are more reluctant to levy high taxes, especially taxes on income and wealth which, by definition, fall most heavily on their upper income supporters.

In a fine contribution to the Royal Commission on the Economic Union and Development Prospects for Canada, David Wolfe (1985, pp.141-142) claimed that "Canada certainly fits the case suggested by David Cameron, in that the federal government has been dominated by a centrist government for most of the postwar period. A closer examination of the politics of taxing and spending in the past decade suggests that the policies adopted by the federal government in Canada parallel those of other centrist and rightist governments". He then went on to carefully list all the tax reductions that the federal Liberal government under Pierre Trudeau began introducing in 1971, reductions that mainly benefited the business and relatively privileged part of the Liberals' national constituency.

Summarizing the results of his study, Wolfe wrote,

> The analysis of the various sources of the deficit presented in this paper indicates that the root of the problem lies with the revenue budget, rather than the expenditure budget. During the period in which the federal government made

an explicit commitment to restrain the growth of expenditures, from late 1975 to the onset of the recession in 1981,
it was highly successful in achieving this goal. ...The government has not enjoyed the same degree of success in its
efforts to stem the revenue loss through tax expenditures.
As the analysis of the tax reform process makes clear, there
are large and powerful political constituencies of centrist
and rightist political parties that can use their political
influence to block such reforms. ...Any attempt to reduce
the deficit through a strategy of tax reform is filled with
political pitfalls. The comparative analysis presented in this
paper suggests that a social democratic government would
be more likely to succeed in the implementation of such a
strategy, but the prospects of this occurring in Canada in
the near future do not appear great. ...However, the failure
to take decisive action presents even greater hazards.
...Attempts to reduce the deficit through the attenuation of
universal social programs or the introduction of regressive
taxes may generate increased social tensions that will
undermine governmental efforts to facilitate long-run struc-
tural adjustments. The necessary course of action is clear;
all that is required is the political will to act. (1985, pp.154-
155)

From our current place in time, the last two sentences are particularly
interesting. We have had significant "attenuation of universal social
programs and the introduction of regressive taxes", the GST (the federal Goods and Services Tax) in particular, but nowhere near the level
of "increased social tensions" one might have expected. Indeed, most
of "the political will to act" since Wolfe published his essay has been
demonstrated by right-wing governments determined to and incredi-
bly successful at pushing through their expected agenda with, I
should add, largely expected results. Rice and Prince (1993, pp.411-
412) poignantly described these results as follows, referring to the
period beginning with the election of Brian Mulroney's Progressive
Conservative government in 1984.

During this period, there has been a decline in the living
conditions of many Canadians. Families are under greater
economic pressure, more children are living in poverty, the
unemployment rate is up, more young people have lost the
will to look for work, there are fewer new, full-time jobs and
housing is harder to find. The result is that more people are
falling into and through the social safety net. One of the
costs of the changes that have taken place during the
Conservative era [and the Liberal era since the federal election of 1993] has been a reduction in social integration. The

> stark differences between the 'haves' and the 'have nots'
> have been highlighted by the removal of universal pro-
> grams. More and more, individuals have been made to feel
> like failures within the postindustrial society. ...While this
> reinforces a neo-conservative agenda, it has long-term impli-
> cations. ...By lowering the safety net and weakening Canada's
> nationhood, the Canadian government is taking one more
> step towards being unable to solve social problems in this
> country.

H. Mimoto and P. Cross (1991) pressed Wolfe's research program forward another five years, leading to practically the same conclusion
reached by Wolfe. "Broadly speaking," they wrote,

> government spending as a share of GDP did not rise signifi-
> cantly over the whole period from 1975 [to 1990]; in fact, it
> moderated compared to the preceding ten years, when social
> programs proliferated. ...Excluding the cost of unemploy-
> ment insurance, which is intended to be self-financing over
> the business cycle, social program spending has not
> increased relative to GDP over the last 16 years. ...Deficits
> became steadily larger after 1975-76 initially more from a
> shortfall originated in numerous changes designed to reduce
> taxes and in the transfer of tax points to the provinces.
> ...higher debt charges accounted for the bulk (70%) of the
> increase in spending relative to GDP from the base period
> [1974-75]. (1991, pp.3.1-3.9)

While the Mimoto and Cross study became the subject of criticisms
by members of the federal Finance Department, Bloskie (1989)
reached similar conclusions and several independent reviewers of the
study found it entirely acceptable (Russell 1991). Several other independent researchers have recently reached the same conclusion;
Gillespie (1991, 1996), Fortin (1996), McCracken (1996) and
Rosenbluth (1996). In fact, every year since 1986 the federal government has had an operating surplus for all government programs and
administration, and the higher debt charges are primarily the direct
result of the Bank of Canada's tight monetary policy (Biddell 1993;
Cohen 1994; Canadian Centre for Policy Alternatives; Choices: A
Coalition for Social Justice 1996; Pope 1996; McCracken 1996). After
reviewing his results from several simulations, McCracken (1996,
p.89) summarized their meaning as follows.

> The essential message of these simulations is that the
> Canadian economy could have followed a different path
> from 1989 to 1995, which would have kept more people

working, business investment higher and fiscal positions of governments under less strain. The governor of the Bank of Canada, with the concurrence of the minister of finance, chose a restrictive monetary policy, with the benefit of a reduction of less than one percentage point in inflation, at the expense of higher unemployment, lower output and large increases in debt ratios.

Consequently, along with progressive tax reforms, the solution of Canada's debt problem must begin with the Bank's policy. This seems to be the case in other OECD countries too, according to Kaul and Langmore (1996, p.259) and Felix (1996a, p.27). Among others, Bradfield (1994) claimed that the Bank of Canada must at least return to its practice (abandoned in the early 1970s) of holding roughly 20% of federal debt, compared to its current holdings of 6%. To prevent inflation, the Bank would also have to raise the reserve requirements for commercial banks, which were reduced to zero in 1994. Other parts of the solution can be found in the *Alternative Federal Budget 1996* (Canadian Centre for Policy Alternatives, jointly with Choices, 1996). The rest of this book will focus on two closely related progressive tax reforms.

Bretton Woods and
Foreign Currency Exchange Activity

he Agreement made among the industrialized nations at Bretton Woods in 1944 was designed to stabilize currency exchange rates in order to ensure that there would be "relatively free multilateral trade and long-term investment after the [Second World] war" (Felix, 1995, p.2). All parties to the Agreement fixed their exchange rates to the US dollar, while the United States in turn fixed its rates to gold. The International Monetary Fund (IMF) was to serve as an international lender of last resort and as an enforcer of the Agreement for any party that was tempted to renege on its commitment. In August 1971 the heart of the Agreement was effectively broken when President Richard Nixon announced that US dollars would no longer be automatically convertible into gold, and the value of international currencies began to float freely in international markets. In 1976 the IMF Articles of Agreement were officially amended to accommodate the floating regime that developed after 1971 (Grabbe 1996, p.32).

Felix (1995, p.5, Table 1) provided an excellent summary of nine key economic performance indicators for the G-7 countries comparing the Bretton Woods period from 1959-1970 to the free floating period from 1974-1989. In every case, the average performance of these countries was superior in the former period. For examples, the average inflation rates, real growth rates and long term interest rates in the former period were 3.9, 4.5 and 6.1, compared to 7.2, 2.2 and 10.3, respectively, in the latter period. Granting that "Post-war reconstruction doubtless contributed to the superior economic performance of the Bretton Woods era" (Felix 1995, p.6), there is no evidence that the floating rate system had any advantages for the real economy. Tobin made similarly critical remarks about the "floating rate system" at the Canadian Centre for Policy Alternatives, but granted that "Speculation on currencies occurs in both regimes" (Tobin 1995, p.3). In his *post mortem* discussion of the 1992-93 crisis in the European Exchange Rate Mechanism, Svensson (1994, pp.462-467) essentially agreed with Tobin's last remark and concluded,

I think we should acknowledge that fixed exchange rates have proved to be much more fragile and difficult to maintain than many of us thought. The increased international capital mobility has made them more vulnerable to speculative attack. ...Therefore, monetary stability and credibility has to be built at home with other means. A move to flexible exchange rates makes it no less essential for a price stability policy to build monetary credibility.

This should not be interpreted as an argument that flexible exchange rates are always to be preferred to fixed exchange rates. There are other arguments than price stability for fixed exchange rates, for instance the reduction of relative price variability in order to promote trade, foreign direct investment and general economic integration.

Block (1996, pp.31-32) took a much harder line on floating rates and finally zeroed in on the sheer size of daily foreign exchange activity. "The experiment with floating rates has been a failure," he wrote.

The currency markets were supposed to get exchange rates 'right,' but this has simply not happened. The markets have a strong tendency to overshoot—to push rates either higher or lower than any analysis of fundamentals would suggest were appropriate. Moreover, the high levels of volatility that have come with floating rates have further intensified the attractiveness of currency speculation and intensified destabilizing capital flows. There are a number of attractive models for fixed exchange rates that would be more flexible than the Bretton Woods system, such as systems that allow currencies to float within a narrow but adjustable band. However, no exchange rate regime will work when more than $1 trillion changes hands every day in the foreign exchange markets.

The following quotation from Kodres (1996, pp.23-23) clearly illustrates the impact of floating rates on foreign exchange activity.

A typical dealing institution writes between 3,000 and 4,000 trading tickets for foreign exchange transactions during an average 24 hour day, and about 50 percent more than that on a busy day. Quoted prices can change 20 times a minute for major currencies, with the dollar-deutsche mark rate changing up to 18,000 times during a single day. During periods of extreme stress, a single dealer may execute a trade every two to four minutes. Single transactions worth between $200 million and $500 million are not uncommon in the foreign exchange market and, at most times, do not affect prices.

Bretton Woods and Foreign Currency Exchange Activity

In their overview of the collection of articles in *The Tobin Tax*, Kaul, Grunberg and Haq (1996, p.3), gave the following account of the relative size of the global foreign currency exchange market.

> Up fourteenfold since 1972, the $1.3 trillion in daily foreign exchange trading registered in 1995 has grown by 50% since 1992, and by 30% if the dollar's depreciation is taken into account. Whatever the statistic chosen, foreign exchange trading is of tremendous proportion. By comparison, the annual global turnover in equity markets in 1995 was $21 trillion—equivalent to just 17 days of trading on the foreign exchange market. The annual global trade in goods and services was a mere $4.3 trillion—or 3.5 days of trading on the foreign exchange market.

According to Frankel (1996, p.46), the Bank for International Settlements's 1995 estimated daily foreign currency exchange trading figure of $1,300 billion included derivative contracts (i.e., contracts involving assets 'derived' from others, as for example, financial futures and options contracts to buy or sell foreign currency at a future time). When derivatives are excluded, the trading figure drops slightly to $1,230 billion a day. Multiplying the $1,300 billion daily figure by 240 business days yields a yearly figure of $312 trillion (Tobin 1996, p.xvi).

Summarizing the scope of foreign currency exchange (FOREX) activity in the 1977 to 1992 period, Felix (1995, pp.15-17) claimed that by the latter year annual net global trading was worth "an astonishing $220 trillion, whereas global exports as a percent of FOREX trading declined from a sizeable 28.5% in 1977 to a minuscule 1.7% in 1992". Furthermore, he estimated that "In 1992,...over 81% of global FOREX transactions were for round trips of seven days or less", and "central banks were probably involved in less than 10% of the global FOREX transactions that year".

In a later study, Felix (1996, p.294) indicated that in 1995 virtually all of the foreign currency exchange transactions in the world were handled in 18 countries, namely, the United Kingdom (30%), United States (16%), Japan (10%), Singapore (7%), Hong Kong (6%), Switzerland (5%), Germany (5%), France (4%), Australia (3%), Denmark, Canada, Belgium and the Netherlands (2% each), Italy, Sweden, Luxembourg, Spain and Austria (1% each). Excluding derivatives and cross-border double counting, he estimated (p.293) that the total net daily turnover that year included 43% spot transactions (i.e., foreign currency exchange deals settled in fewer than 3 days), 8% outright forwards (i.e., deals settled in 3 or more days), and 49% swaps (i.e., exchanges of one currency for another on one day, matched by reverse exchanges on a later day).

According to Walmsley (1992, p.41), "Participants in the market consist of five main groups: central banks, commercial banks, other financial institutions, corporate customers, and brokers. By far the largest volume of trading is conducted by commercial banks ... In the corporate sector, the two largest trading groups have traditionally been the oil companies and commodity companies".

Given the incredible size of global economic activity connected to financial transactions, it is no wonder that such activity would attract the attention of governments and others with an interest in its sustainability. In the next chapter I review some of the most salient literature concerned with tapping this activity as a source of revenue and providing regulation that would still allow legitimate activities to continue.

The Idea of a Tobin Tax

"Among the proposals for greater control over foreign exchange markets..." Langmore (1995, p.191) listed "strengthened requirements for the provision of information; tighter prudential controls over all financial institutions, not merely banks; compulsory non-interest-bearing deposits with central banks related to the size of foreign exchange purchases; capital charges on the net foreign exchange positions of financial institutions; and a transactions levy on all international financial flows". As one might have expected, Langmore claimed that it is most likely that some combination of all these options would finally be required, and I would certainly support this view. In fact, all the best sources that I found for information regarding the control of foreign currency exchange markets recommended a broad mixture of policies; e.g., Griffith-Jones (1996), Eichengreen and Wyplosz (1996), Folkerts-Landau and Ito (1995), Guttmann (1989), Tobin (1974).

In 1978 the Nobel Laureate, James Tobin, re-introduced his own version of a transactions levy, following up a suggestion made by J.M. Keynes, which has since become known as "the Tobin tax". Focusing his attention on the US market, Keynes (1936, pp.159-160) pointed out that "It is usually agreed that casinos should in the public interest be inaccessible and expensive. And perhaps the same is true of stock exchanges. ...The introduction of a substantial government transfer tax on all transactions might prove the most serviceable reform available, with a view to mitigating the predominance of speculation over enterprise in the US". While Keynes apparently recognized that the foreign currency exchange market should also be subject to the tax (Eichengreen, Tobin and Wyplosz 1995), his emphasis seems to have been on internal financial transactions while that of Tobin has been on foreign currency exchange transactions.

Tobin (1978, p.154) explained the problem as he saw it as follows.

> ...the mobility of financial capital limits viable differences among national interest rates and thus severely restricts the ability of central banks and governments to pursue monetary and fiscal policies appropriate to their internal economies.

Likewise speculation on exchange rates, whether its consequences are vast shifts of official assets and debts or large movements of exchange rates themselves, have serious and frequently painful real internal economic consequences. Domestic policies are relatively powerless to escape them or offset them. ...Prices in goods and labor markets move much more sluggishly, in response to excess supply and demand, than the prices of financial assets, including exchange rates.

Given this view of the problem, he went on to say that his

... specific proposal is actually not new. I offered it in 1972 in my Janeway Lectures at Princeton, published in 1974 as The New Economics One Decade Older, pp.88-92. The idea fell like a stone in a deep well. If I cast it in the water again, it is because events since the first try have strengthened my belief that something of the sort needs to be done. The proposal is an internationally uniform tax on all spot conversions of one currency into another, proportional to the size of the transaction. The tax would particularly deter short-term financial round- trip excursions into another currency. A 1% tax, for example, could be overcome only by an 8 point differential in the annual yields of Treasury bills or Eurocurrency deposits denominated in dollars or Deutschmarks. The corresponding differential for one-year maturities would be 2 points. A permanent investment in another country or currency area, with regular repatriation of yield when earned, would need a 2% advantage in marginal efficiency over domestic investment.

As a result of many years of thought and critical debate, the latest version of Tobin's proposal is more sophisticated than his first version. In the latest version, Eichengreen, Tobin and Wyplosz (1995, pp.165-166) explain its essential elements as follows.

A transactions tax on purchases and sales of foreign exchange would have to be [1] universal and [2] uniform: it would [3] have to apply to all jurisdictions, and [4] the rate would have to be equalized across markets. Were it imposed unilaterally by one country, that country's FOREX market would simply move offshore ... [5] Enforcement of the universal tax would depend principally on major banks and on the jurisdictions that regulate them. [6] The surveillance of national regulatory authorities could be the responsibility of a multilateral agency like the Bank for International Settlements or the International Monetary Fund. It might be authorised to set the size of the tax within limits. [7] It would have to possess sanctions that could be levied on countries that fail to comply with the measure.

The Idea of a Tobin Tax

A review of the literature surrounding the Tobin tax since 1978 in the light of the seven enumerated features in the preceding paragraph clearly reveals that the current advocates of the tax have taken their critics seriously. Although some of Tobin's remarks about his tax (e.g., Canadian Centre for Policy Alternatives 1995) suggest that the Tobin tax is a species of financial transactions tax which is levied on only one of many kinds of financial instruments, he clearly intended a much broader tax at least since 1978. Near the end of that paper, he wrote: "The tax would apply to all purchases of financial instruments denominated in another currency – from currency and coin to equity securities. It would have to apply, I think, to all payments in one currency for goods, services, and real assets sold by a resident of another currency area. I don't intend to add even a small barrier to trade. But I see offhand no other way to prevent financial transactions disguised as trade" (p.159). Presumably, all or most of the tax would be paid for by purchasers of financial instruments, either directly and explicitly or indirectly as part of sellers' fees.

Rudiger Dornbusch (1990, p.43) considered Tobin's idea of a uniform tax on all foreign currency exchange transactions and concluded,

> There is no reason only to tax foreign exchange transactions. Since asset market instability suggests short-horizon speculation in all asset markets the response should be a world-wide financial transactions tax. A moderate worldwide tax on all financial transactions would force asset markets to take a long-run view of the assets they price. As a result there would be more stabilising speculation. The case for such a tax is becoming more and more apparent after the crash of 1987.

A similar sort of broad financial transactions tax was recently recommended by J.L. Biddell and Jordan Grant (1994, pp.1-2). In particular, they

> ... proposed that a one-tenth of one percent transaction tax be levied upon the sale or transfer of all Canadian dollar denominated financial instruments - stocks, bonds, treasury bills, bankers acceptances, commercial paper, other money market instruments, options, futures and derivatives. ...one of the principle benefits of such a tax would be to slow down the flows of very short-term 'hot' money flowing into and out of the Canadian economy. This would help to stabilize the daily fluctuations in interest rates and exchange rates, and encourage longer-term, more stable investing.

GOOD TAXES

A tax rate of one-tenth of one percent on the $21 trillion of transactions reported in the Canadian Depository for Securities for 1995 would have produced about $21 billion, which would have been enough to make the GST superfluous. Following explanatory remarks on their proposal, Biddell and Grant wrote: "Currently, financial transactions go untaxed. If the government is considering a tax on gambling winnings, it should consider taxing the biggest casino of all - the financial markets" (p.1). Tobin (1984, p.5) also commented on the casino-like character of these markets, referring to the work of Alfred Cowles in 1933 which has "been confirmed many times in different ways". According to Powers (1993, p.24), among commodity traders in general, "All studies conducted over the years on this topic yield the same conclusion: most individual traders lose. Studies done by the University of Illinois and others, as well as private industry surveys, have concluded that overall about twice as many people lose money as make money. ...On the average each loser lost more than each winner made." Later (p.54) he added, "If you have a family and a net worth of less than $200,000, you probably should not be trading."

While Biddell and Grant's arithmetic leading to the potential $21 billion in tax revenues is clear, it is not clear that actual revenues from a financial transactions excise tax in Canada would reach that amount. Authors of the Library of Parliament (1996) review of such taxes were pretty clearly biased against them, but they also thought there would be relatively little revenue generated. Their estimates ran from a low of about $300 million to a high of about $10.6 billion, with $327 million as their best guess of the total "net revenues" (Library of Parliament 1996, p.24). Interested readers will have to study the assumptions connected to these estimates and others in order to decide for themselves what revenues should be expected from such taxes. Personally, I suspect we might reach a figure somewhere between $10 billion and $20 billion from a broad-based tax.

The Independent Commission on Population and Quality of Life (1996, pp.281-284) also recommended a broad financial transactions tax. In the Commission's view,

> Given the interlinkages existing among the various sub-markets — those of currency exchange, securities and bonds, stock-shares, and derivatives—it is advisable not to deal with each of these market segments in isolation.
>
> For this reason the Commission recommends that a flat transaction charge should be levied uniformly, equally, and universally on all present and future types of financial transaction occurring in the globalized market-place. If the levy were fixed at a rate of 0.01 per cent of each transaction, the potential yield is estimated to exceed, conservatively speak-

ing, $150 billion annually. ...The fee charged would have to be collected by national central banks, and collection would be required of every member of the IMF or the World Bank as a condition of receiving loans from them. The proceeds of the collection could be deposited in a Global Priority Fund, for example, under the auspices of the BIS [Bank for International Settlements]. Other institutional solutions are possible.

Addressing the perceived problem that "a small charge on international financial transactions would not create distortions but would also fail to inhibit speculative behavior in foreign exchange markets", Spahn (1996, pp.26-27) suggested,

> A possible compromise would be a two-tier structure: a minimal-rate transaction tax and an exchange surcharge that, as an antispeculation device, would be triggered only during periods of exchange rate turbulence and on the basis of well-established quantitative criteria. ...
>
> A minimal nominal charge of, for example, two basis points [i.e., 0.02%] on foreign exchange transactions would raise the cost of capital insignificantly and would probably have no effect on the volume of transactions involving currency conversions. A transaction tax could also be imposed on derivative trades at half the standard rate, or one basis point. This would allow the derivatives markets to continue functioning at low cost while preventing the use of derivatives to evade taxes. ...
>
> The exchange surcharge would be administered in conjunction with the underlying transaction tax, but its aim and implementation would be different. The aim would be to tax negative externalities associated with excessive volatility. For normal operations, the fixed-rate surcharge would be zero because the tax base is zero, which assures market liquidity and allows efficient trading. The surcharge would be levied only during periods of speculative trading when the tax base becomes positive. It could be confined to cash transactions or, if necessary, could easily be extended to the derivative market. Ideally, if the exchange surcharge achieves its objective, it would generate no revenues. ...
>
> Ideally, the two-tier scheme would work on a global scale, as would the tax originally proposed by Tobin, but, initially, it could be implemented unilaterally by one or a few countries.

A more detailed account of his proposal is given in Spahn (1995, pp.31-38).

GOOD TAXES

Mendez (1995, pp.25-27) proposed another alternative to a Tobin tax in the form of a Global Foreign Currency Exchange (FXE). In his own words,

> Because it would be a free-market mechanism, the exchange would avoid most of the political and practical obstacles facing the Tobin tax. At the same time, it could generate substantial funds for global governance and international public goods.
>
> The rationale for such an exchange stems from the fact that the present market is disorganized and actually consists of two markets: an inside interbank market, where competition is keen and the best prices prevail, and the publicly quoted market to which end users—importers, exporters, portfolio managers, industrial corporations, tourists, and other individuals—have access, but only at inflated prices. This difference exists despite the fact that transaction costs in both markets are identical, in view of the vast amounts involved in each transaction, whether between banks or between banks and most end users. (This does not apply to individuals going to retail intermediaries, where transactions are small and costlier.)
>
> The FXE...would serve the foreign currency market in the same way that national bourses or securities exchanges provide orderly markets for stocks and bonds. ...FXE's revenue potential is enormous. ...On the basis of a total market of $1 trillion,... . If FXE captured 70 per cent...[with]...fees or commissions...set at a very low rate: a .1 per cent rate, for example, would yield $84 million daily, and a 1 per cent rate would yield 10 times that amount, or $840 million a day. These rates would be less than the premiums most end users pay in the current two-tier market.

Considering a general "securities trading tax" for the United States (i.e., an excise tax), Baker, Pollin and Schaberg (1994, p.623) claimed,

> The potential benefits of [such a] tax can be appreciated only in terms of the magnitude of the financial markets. ...Trading volume of existing securities is enormous: in 1992, $3.1 trillion in the stock market; $8.2 trillion in the corporate bond market; $44.4 trillion in the government securities market. By comparison, the US economy's total output of goods and services (GDP) in 1992 was $6 trillion. In other words, trading on all three markets—a total of $55.7 trillion—was nearly ten times greater than the economy's output that year. More to the point, new issues were minuscule relative to trading volume. Considering just the stock market, the ratio of trading volume to new funds raised...means that $113.80 in stock trades took

place for every dollar raised to finance new corporate investments.

According to Summers and Summers (1990, pp.153-168),

> Fifty years after Keynes, the US today is one of the only major industrialized countries [Canada is another] which does not levy a significant excise tax on the transfer of financial securities. Such taxes raised more than $12 billion in Japan in 1987, and several billion in the United Kingdom [US $1,300 million in 1993 according to Griffith-Jones 1996, p.146] despite its smaller stock market capitalization. ...Most major industrialized countries impose some form of STET [Securities Transaction Excise Tax]. ...these transaction taxes are in place in West Germany, France, Italy, the Netherlands, Sweden, Switzerland, the United Kingdom, and Japan, among other places. They represent a significant amount of revenue: in 1985, revenue collected ranged from .04 percent of Gross National Product in Germany to .48 percent of Gross National Product in Switzerland. This corresponds to a range of $2 billion to $25 billion in the United States. ...A comparison of the administrative approaches used in other countries suggests a number of possible ways to structure a STET. The overall lesson to be drawn from comparisons is that a STET can be made to work in a modern financial economy without insurmountable distortions, and without crippling the nation's securities industry.

In fact, the United States did have an excise tax on "the issuance and transfer of stocks and certificates of indebtedness issued by a corporation" from 1914 to 1965, which included some exemptions for government and building loans, and transfers by reason of death and bankruptcy (Joint Committee on Taxation 1990, p.7). More recently, according to Schwert and Seguin (1993, p.28),

> As early as 1982, Congress considered a fee of 6 cents for each futures contract bought and sold on an organized exchange. Although the Bush administration, in its 1991 budget, proposed an 11 cents fee for futures trades, this fee never passed Congress. Proposals for a 13 cents fee in the 1992 budget and a 15 cents fee in the 1993 budget also failed in Congress. The Clinton administration is currently proposing a 14 cents fee.
> The 1990 budget negotiations considered a securities transaction excise tax (STET) of 0.5% on all financial transactions except Treasury securities, but this was not included in the final budget agreement. The proposal (hereafter referred to as the "0.5% broad-based STT") would have applied to

trades of stocks, bonds, notes, partnership interests, options and futures contracts. Under the proposal, all sellers would pay the tax, regardless of domicile or tax status.

The proposal described in the preceding paragraph is fairly close to the Biddell and Grant proposal. Schwert and Seguin are not supporters of such taxes, and they found it interesting that

> none of the proposals for an STT has suggested that the primary or secondary markets for Treasury securities should be covered by a new transaction tax. This suggests that the US government recognizes that increasing transaction costs for the securities it sells to finance its own activities would raise the cost of borrowing, especially in the case of short-term securities such as Treasury bills and notes. ...it is curious that government would exempt only its own securities from a broad-based transaction tax. This seems to imply that legislators and regulators understand the potentially large indirect costs of such taxes, but do not mind imposing those costs on other issuers of securities (p.34).

I suppose legislators and regulators do understand that an STT would entail increased costs for traders. However, it seems perfectly reasonable to tax for-profit traders but not the government. Because for-profit trading would not be sustainable without government services (e.g., maintaining the integrity of the national and international financial systems) those who profit from those services cannot be allowed to take a free ride on the public purse. On the other hand, because a tax on government securities trading would simply increase the cost of having government services, it would be counter-productive for governments to both sell and tax the sale of their own securities. As a matter of fact, in Taiwan government bonds are excluded from the securities transactions tax, while in Austria they are taxed at a lower rate than dividend bearing securities (Spahn 1995, pp.51-54).

Arguments in Favour of
Taxing Financial Transactions

s the following list demonstrates, a wide variety of arguments in support of a Tobin tax in particular and financial transactions taxes in general have appeared in the literature. Generally speaking, I try to present proponents' and opponents' views in their own words. However, lest there be any misunderstanding, some of the strongest opponents of such taxes (e.g., Folkerts-Landau, Ito, Hubbard, Brockway and Hakkio) have often formulated crisp accounts of proponent's arguments and some of the strongest proponents of such taxes (e.g., Tobin, Felix, Stiglitz, Summers and Summers), have often formulated crisp accounts of opponents' objections. Below one can usually distinguish proponents and opponents from the total context of the discussion.

The 19 arguments in favour of some sort of financial transactions taxes are as follows.

1. "Currently the power of central banks to intervene on world money markets is circumscribed by the fact that speculators have larger pools of cash to manipulate than do all the world's central banks put together. Since the central banks themselves would not have to pay the tax and the speculators would, national monetary authorities would enjoy a double advantage. A lower volume of transactions would reduce the amount a central bank would have to spend to defend its currency" (Ecumenical Coalition for Economic Justice 1995, p.6). Similar arguments may be found in Felix (1995) pp.42, 55, and Kaul, Grunberg and Haq (1996) p.4. This argument apparently assumes that central banks would refrain from speculating in FOREX markets.

2. "The Tobin tax is now firmly on the international agenda" (Ecumenical Coalition for Economic Justice 1995, p.6). According to Tobin (Canadian Centre for Policy Alternatives 1995, p.11), "...the United Nations Development Program is laying on quite a substantial research program ... looking more deeply into the technicalities of

universalizing it and enforcing it". A great deal of the output from the UNDP's efforts so far were published in Haq, Kaul and Grunberg (1996), which is a collection of articles from a conference of experts held in October 1995. Inge Kaul, the Director of the UNDP's Office of Development Studies, argued that for purposes of funding the operations of global governance,

> The most obvious place to look for global funding sources are the use of global *commons* (e.g., oceanic seabeds or the air) and globalized *activities* (e.g., foreign currency movements and trade, especially trade in global 'bads' such as exports of arms and dumping of toxic wastes. ...If there were the requisite political will among UN member states 'to go global' in terms of the organization's financing, there would be no scarcity of funds. On the contrary, there would be much more money than the UN is likely to require for its own purposes in the foreseeable future (Kaul 1995, pp.186-187).

Tobin (1996, p.xi) also claimed that Stanley Fischer, First Deputy Managing Director of the IMF, agreed that a Tobin tax would be "a potentially useful measure if enforcement problems could be solved". Langmore (1995, p.193) mentioned the UNDP's efforts as well as those by the International Labour Organization, the Commission on Global Governance, and some other individual efforts. The Independent Commission on Population and Quality of Life (1996) which met several times from 1991 to 1995, concluded that "the most promising source of finance for global priorities, in terms of yield, would be an international charge on all transactions in the world's financial markets: currencies, bonds and other securities, derivatives, and stock shares" (p.281). Much of the International Monetary Fund's publication, *International Capital Markets Developments, Prospects, and Policy Issues* (Folkerts-Landau and Ito 1995) is devoted to detailed analyses of versions of financial transfer taxes and other means of controlling international capital flows including empirical studies of countries in which various tactics have actually been employed.

3. "Although powerful financial interests oppose the Tobin tax, the US government itself has a strong interest in pursuing a measure that would allow it to regain more control over its own monetary policy" (Ecumenical Coalition for Economic Justice 1995, p.6). According to Tobin (1995, p.6), "the principal purpose of the proposed tax is to expand the autonomy of national monetary policies". Langmore (1995, p.192) and Kaul, Grunberg and Haq (1996, p.4) make the same point.

4. There are a number of different estimates of the amount of revenue that might be obtained from a global Tobin tax, because researchers make different assumptions about the elasticity of foreign currency exchange demand, the average pre-tax costs of foreign exchange transactions and the likely amount of tax evasion. Nevertheless, all of the estimates are relatively big and there is some convergence of views from different investigators. Following the 1995 conference, Tobin (1996, p.xvii) expressed the view that "...the tax rate must be lower than I originally thought. It should not exceed 0.25% and perhaps should be as low as 0.1%. Otherwise, the tax would swamp the normal commission charged".

Frankel (1996, p.61) claimed, "A typical transaction cost for foreign exchange might be 0.1%. (This is a generous estimate, applicable to a trade between a bank and a corporate customer. The actual number is likely to be much smaller for interdealer trading [i.e., "wholesale" trading (Kenen 1996, p.110)], which is the majority of trading currently.) So, a charge of 0.1% would constitute at least a doubling of the current transaction cost". Frankel's estimates are consistent with those of Felix and Sau (1996, p.231), and below I assume these estimates are accurate when I consider likely revenues obtainable from a Tobin tax. If Spahn (1995, p.12) was right when he claimed that "Large institutional investors routinely engage in short-term arbitrage transactions for margins as little as 3 to 5 basis points [i.e., 0.03% to 0.05%] on highly liquid transactions (such as US-dollar-DM swap)", then even a 0.05% tax rate might be too high. However, the impression I get from the estimates of Frankel, Felix and Sau is that 0.05% is a reasonable rate, all things considered.

In estimating the global tax base for a Tobin tax, Felix and Sau (1996, p.228) began by subtracting "10% of the $220 trillion [mentioned above for 1992] to account for official, and presumably tax exempt, FOREX transactions" and another "25% of the $220 trillion to account for private transactions that elude the tax by one means or another", which would leave a global base of about $144 trillion. Felix (1995, p.41) estimated that, beginning with a $144 trillion global tax base in 1992, a phased-in 0.25% Tobin tax would have generated from about $172 billion to $283 billion annually by the fourth year of its existence. Felix's own and Felix and Sau's assumptions and models are presented with enough detail that one can make adjustments to them to suit one's own assessments of reality.

Felix and Sau (1996, pp.238-240) estimated global revenues running from about $302 billion to $393 billion in 1995 from a

0.25% tax, from about $148 billion to $180 billion from a 0.1% tax, and from about $90 billion to $97 billion from a 0.05% tax. Kenen (1996, p.110) estimated that a global tax of 5 basis points (i.e., 0.05%) would have generated about $100 billion in 1992, which is bigger than Felix and Sau's (1996, p.240) estimates of from $61 billion to $66 billion for the same year and tax rate. Frankel (1996, p.63) estimated that a global tax of 0.1% would have generated about $166 billion in 1992, which is also bigger than Felix and Sau's (1996, p.239) estimates of from $101 billion to $122 billion for the same year and tax rate. As indicated above, the Independent Commission on Population and Quality of Life (1996, p.282) estimated that a 0.01% global tax would have generated about $150 billion in 1992.

For our purposes, it is sufficient to focus on the most modest of all these estimates and to notice the enormous potential revenue available. "In its 1994 Human Development Report the UNDP estimated that the cost of wiping out the worst forms of poverty in the world by providing basic energy, water and sanitation for the most needy would be between $30 and $40 billion a year" (Ecumenical Coalition for Economic Justice 1995, p.7). So, on the basis of Felix and Sau's most modest estimates, the global revenue of a 0.05% Tobin tax in 1995 would have been two to three times as great as what would have been required to eliminate the world's worst forms of poverty. No wonder, then, that in the UNDP's *Human Development Report 1994* (pp.68-69), a Tobin tax was recommended as one source of funding for "global human security compacts" regarding things such as natural disasters, ethnic conflicts and environmental pollution. In Langmore's view (1995, p.192), one of the main benefits of the tax is that "Part of the revenue could also be used for establishing a permanent, reliable source of funding for the United Nations system at last. ...Revenue received by the UN could be used for disaster relief, security and development. There would be widespread support for the establishment of a permanent disaster relief fund...". That view is also shared by Walker (1993), Frankel (1996), and Kaul and Langmore (1996).

Having come so far reviewing the various estimates of the global tax revenue obtainable from a Tobin tax, it is perhaps worthwhile to provide estimates of the revenue obtainable to each of major dealing countries. Using Felix and Sau's (1996, p.240) estimates for the annual revenue from a 0.05% tax applied to 1995 foreign currency exchange volumes, the distribution in billions of US dollars is as follows:

Industrial Countries

United Kingdom . . . . 28.7 billion
United States 15.1
Japan 9.9
Switzerland. 5.3
Germany. 4.5
France 3.6
Australia 2.4
Denmark. 1.8
Canada 1.7
Netherlands 1.4
Sweden 1.2
Other OECD countries. 8.1

Developing Countries

Singapore 6.4
Hong Kong. 5.5
South Africa. 0.3
Bahrain 0.1

Other Less Developed Countries . 1.1

Total for all countries . . . . **97.1 billion**

Issues related to policies and procedures for distributing the bulk of these funds from the dealing countries to other countries will be considered below.

5. "...the successive governmental bailouts of international financial markets from the crises to which they have become increasingly prone have been raising moral hazard risks, encouraging yet greater speculative flows. This increases the prospect that future crises may exceed the fire-fighting capability of the G-7 monetary authorities" (Felix, 1995, p.1). Tobin made a similar point at the Canadian Centre for Policy Alternatives (1995, p.5). According to Soros (1994, p.104) the bailout of Mexico in 1982 required the joint efforts of the IMF, BIS, "a number of governments and central banks, and a much larger number [over 500] of commercial banks".

Felix (1995, p.37) reported that the IMF identified "eight crises [in the 1973-1989 period] whose spillover threat evoked coordinated international crisis management by the monetary authorities" and he also identified three more in the first half of the nineties. He then ominously warned us that "With the reserves/FOREX ratios dwindling to impotence, and the IMF and G-7 monetary authorities persisting with a crisis management strategy that encourages riskier global financial forays [namely, that some commercial banks and financial markets are too big to be allowed to fail], the likelihood of a future crisis exceeding the crisis management resources of the befuddled monetary authorities is becoming uncomfortably high" (pp.45-46). If one adds to this warning the recent finding that "currency crises appear to pass 'contagiously' from one country to another", the level of discomfort goes even higher (Eichengreen, Rose and Wyplosz 1996, p.iii).

Stiglitz (1993, p.27) is especially lucid on this score.

> Governments cannot sit idly by when faced with the impending collapse of a major financial institution. Moreover, both banks and investors know that the government will step in because it cannot commit itself *not* to intervene in the economy ...
>
> The government thus performs the role of an insurer, whether or not it has explicitly issued a policy. The provision of insurance tends to alter behavior, giving rise to the well-known problem of moral hazard; that is, the insured has a reduced incentive to avoid the insured-against event. In this case, banks, knowing that they are effectively insured, may take greater risks than they otherwise would. In particular, they may undertake risks similar to those being undertaken by other banks, since they assume that although the government might ignore the problems of a single bank, it could not allow the entire financial system to go belly-up. So long as the bank does what other banks are doing, the probability of a rescue is extremely high.
>
> Most insurance gives rise to moral hazard problems. Insurance firms attempt to mitigate the moral hazard problem by imposing restrictions. For instance, fire insurance companies typically require that sprinklers be installed in commercial buildings. Once we recognize the role of government as an insurer (willing or unwilling), financial market regulations can be seen from a new perspective, as akin to the regulations an insurance company imposes. The effects of some versions of financial market liberalization are similar to an insurance company's deciding to abandon fire codes, with similar disastrous consequences.

Because a Tobin tax would be levied on every exchange of foreign currency, it would provide a signal and some incentive for reducing the risk of a global financial crisis. In a later study, Felix and Sau (1996, p.225) pointed out that "Global official reserves are now less than the value of one day of global foreign exchange turnover, a 93 percent decline from 1977".

6. Since there is apparently no groundswell of commitment to control international capital mobility with new regulations, a Tobin tax at least promises to provide the international community with a piece of the pie of profits flowing from such mobility. According to Felix (1995, p.36), current IMF proposals for the G-7 countries to just make some new agreements to control international capital mobility would require "a level of political commitment to exchange rate stability far greater than what was needed to save the Bretton Woods regime during its terminal crisis".

7. Sin taxes on relatively self- and socially-destructive behaviour such as smoking tobacco and drinking alcoholic products are generally accepted as good sources of government revenues, and a Tobin tax is a kind of sin tax since "it penalizes and thus restricts socially undesirable behavior" (Felix 1995, p.39). Similarly, Stiglitz (1989, p.103) remarked that "A turnover tax...can...be viewed as a special and potentially important case of a Pigovian corrective tax, a tax that improves economic efficiency at the same time that it raises revenues". Other examples of Pigovian taxes (named after the British economist A.C. Pigou) include special taxes on polluters of the marine environment, on users of greenhouse gas-producing carbon fuels and on producers of ozone-depleting chlorofluorocarbons, (Mendez, 1992, p.227). Recent work by Goulder, Parry and Burtraw (1996, p.1) suggests that the aggregate social cost of environmental regulation can be reduced when the revenue obtained from such taxes is recycled to "enable the public sector to finance cuts in existing, distortionary taxes [e.g. the GST], thereby avoiding some of the deadweight cost associated with these taxes". A slightly more cautious overview of issues related to such taxes may be found in Oates (1995).

It is perhaps worthwhile to recall here a point made by Brockway (1987, p.3), namely, that those who are using pension funds for relatively high risk, short-term profits may be making "inappropriate" use of funds "intended for retirement use". This was also the view expressed by Brady (1990, p.41). Such use of pension funds became the focus of two legislative proposals in the US Senate. In 1989 the Excessive Churning and Speculation Act (S.1654) was proposed, which would have levied "an excise tax on the short-term capital gains of certain pension funds" and in 1990 the Long-Term Investment, Competitiveness, and Corporate Takeover Reform Act (S.2160) was proposed, which would have prohibited pension plans from turning over securities in less than three months under certain conditions (Joint Committee on Taxation 1990, p.8). As one would imagine, people with a vested interest in pension plans offered consid-

GOOD TAXES

erable resistance to these proposals; e.g., Joint Committee on Taxation (1990), Shultz (1990), McGrath (1990), American Federation of Labor and Congress of Industrial Organizations (1990), Association of Private Pension and Welfare Plans (1990), Public Securities Association (1990). The following remarks from McGrath (1990, p.70) on behalf of the National Association of State Treasurers and the Council of Institutional Investors provide an excellent snapshot of the views of pension managers.

> First, there appears to be a misunderstanding to the basic assumptions of our investment philosophy. We understand that no investors have a more critical need for a long-term perspective than our pension funds. Our fiduciary responsibility under the law is solely to provide promised benefits to our individual members. Secondly, and with this legal burden in mind, we do not madly flip our portfolios over by the minute like short order cooks in a pancake house. ...We pull [turnover] market averages down, not up; and our turnover has decreased in each of the last two years despite dramatically lower transaction costs. Pension funds tend to be long-term investors. To give you one typical example:...the largest public pension fund in the nation, the California Public Employees' Retirement System, has an annual turnover rate of less than five percent and an average holding period of eight years ... Thirdly, finally and most fundamentally: transaction taxes HARM rather than enhance, the health of the economy in both the short and long term.

8. A public good may be defined by either of two characteristics, namely, jointness and nonexclusiveness. Roughly speaking, something has the quality of jointness (or nonrivalrous consumption) if using it does not imply using it up. For example, any number of people may use the same information or knowledge at the same time and virtually forever. Something has the quality of nonexclusiveness if nonpurchasers cannot be excluded from it. For example, if Canada is internationally secure, then all its inhabitants can enjoy that security whether every person pays for it or not. Furthermore, because everyone benefits whether they pay for it or not, self-interested people have a reason to try to avoid paying for it altogether. That is, they have a reason to try to take a free ride on other people's payments. This is the so-called free-rider problem. Insofar as a stable international financial system benefits those who pay as well as those who do not pay for it, it is a public good (Kaul 1995; Mendez 1995) and therefore creates some incentive for people to try to take a free ride on the good behaviour of others. A Tobin tax would address this problem by arresting some of the currency speculation that tends to destabilize

the international financial system. (Felix 1995, p.39), and by forcing speculators and other traders to pay some share of the costs of their activities.

9. Since there is some evidence that export-led development is more energy-intensive and environmentally more destructive than development based on production for domestic markets (Michalos 1997), a Tobin tax would contribute to the creation of a more environmentally sustainable world-wide economic system.

10. "By helping make full employment policies in the industrialized countries viable again, the tax would not merely advance the broader efforts to stabilize the globalized financial system, but would also weaken the neo-mercantilist pressures that motivate much of the current drive for trade expansion, to the detriment of the developing countries. ...demands in the industrial countries for protection against low wage imports would slacken and pressures on the developing countries to open up their markets and lift capital controls would also soften" (Felix 1995, p.48).

11. Compared to regressive consumption taxes like the GST, a Tobin tax would tend to be progressive because relatively low income people would not be involved in the capital transactions captured by the tax. (Biddell and Grant 1994, p.7; Catt 1994, p.2; Ecumenical Coalition for Economic Justice 1995, p.7) According to Summers and Summers (1990a, p.171), in the United States, "More than half of the stock held by individuals is held by those in the top one percent of the wealth distribution". Hakkio (1994, p.29) reported that a 1989 survey in the United States showed that "15 percent of households earning less than $30,000 held stock, 46 percent of households earning between $30,000 and $100,000 held stock, and almost 80 percent of households earning more than $100,000 held stock". In Canada, in 1990 "only 40% of taxfilers with total incomes under $20,000 reported investment income as compared with 92% of taxfilers with incomes of $100,000 or more" (Siroonian 1993, p.3.10). Perhaps even more importantly, for taxfilers with a total median income of $15,700, about 90% of their reported investment income came from interest, while for taxfilers with a total income of $100,000 or more, about 40% came from dividends (Siroonian 1993, p.3.9).

12. According to Langmore (1995, p.192), a Tobin tax would be "electorally popular" because "few people like speculators". In the words of the Ecumenical Coalition for Economic Justice (1995, p.7), "As a levy on Wall Street and Bay Street rather than on Main Street it appeals to the populist streak of many anti-tax protestors". In a roughly similar vein, Brockway (1987, p.2) pointed out that the fact that the tax "would not be paid directly by the population at large (unlike, e.g.,

the income tax), [suggests] there may be less opposition to the STET than to an increase in certain other taxes".

13. By decreasing the volatility of exchange rates and increasing their predictability, a Tobin tax would allow international traders to invest more funds in the production of real goods and less in the protection of their investments from foreign currency exchange market shocks (Block 1996, p.32). According to Felix (1995, pp.22), it was the increased volatility of exchange rates that severely arrested the "growth of domestic output and income around the world" as well as global trade in real goods in the 1983-1992 period. Tobin claimed that "the surprise appreciation of the US dollar against the Japanese yen in the early 1980s nearly destroyed the American automotive industry" (Tobin 1995, p.4), and "The Volcker Commission on the international financial system argued that extreme swings on the foreign exchange markets have been a contributory cause of the low growth in industrial countries since the 1970s" (Langmore 1995, p.190).

"In a world of floating exchange rates," Walker (1993, p.9) wrote, "companies that sell goods abroad would be foolish not to ensure that the foreign currency in which they will be paid on delivery will be worth enough to justify their work. They do this by hedging, buying currency forward, to ensure that they will have a predictable return on their investment." Some hedging, then, would be arrested by a Tobin tax. Regarding the impact of hedging on international trade, Wachtel (1994, p.77) wisely asserted that

> The most fervent advocates of free trade are also the ones that resist most aggressively any efforts to place public policy boundaries around the present foreign exchange markets. But they fail to realize that these arrangements increase the cost of internationally traded goods and, therefore, lower the volume of international trade. Public policy that addresses foreign exchange volatility and speculation is also trade policy in the best tradition of an open trading system shorn of the ideologically driven mantra of 'free trade'.

Wachtel's views were supported in a recent book by Eric Helleiner (1994). Through a careful analysis of international trade and finance from the Bretton Woods agreements to the 1990s, Helleiner demonstrated the powerful roles that states played in creating and continue to play in sustaining the current "liberal international economic order", and how ambiguous that "order" really is. Most importantly for our purposes, Helleiner (1994, p.20) showed that

> As policy makers noted in the early postwar years, a liberal international financial order is not necessarily compatible

with a liberal international trading order. The Bretton Woods negotiators worried that speculative and disequilibrating capital movements would disrupt trade patterns and encourage protectionist pressures. Recent experience has to some extent borne out these fears. Many observers have attributed the increase in restrictive trade practices in the 1970s and 1980s to the globalization of financial markets. Robert Gilpin [1987, p.367] has argued that 'as international finance has more tightly integrated national markets, states have responded by increasing the level of trade protectionism'. Similarly, Rimmer De Vries [1990, p.9] concluded in 1990 that 'there is a certain tension in maintaining both free capital and free trade'. In this sense, the difference in state behavior in trade and finance lends strength to the assertion that different parts of a liberal international economic order are not necessarily compatible.

14. Summers and Summers (1990, pp.154-165) question the ability of US, and by implication, Canadian financial markets to "perform their ultimate social functions: spreading risks, guiding the investment of scarce capital, and processing and disseminating the information possessed by diverse traders. ...It is hard to believe," they wrote, "that investments made with a horizon of hours reveal much socially-beneficial information to a marketplace. A transaction tax is a natural policy for alleviating this market failure. ...By encouraging investment research directed at long-term rather than short-term prediction, a transaction tax might help to solve the conflict noted by Keynes between the privately and socially most desirable investment strategies". Tornell (1990) took a similar line with a relatively more formal model, and Shleifer and Summers (1990, p.24) addressed the issue from a more behaviouristic perspective as follows.

A look at how market participants behave provides perhaps the most convincing evidence that noise rather than information drives many of their decisions. Investors follow market gurus and forecasters, such as Joe Granville and 'Wall Street Week.' Charging bulls, Jimmy Connors and John Houseman all affect where and how people entrust their money. When Merrill Lynch changed from their charging bulls ad (filmed in Mexico) to a single bull ad ('a breed apart'), many more people chose to take their advice. Financial gurus that attract large followings never claim to have access to inside information. Rather, they insist that they are following reliable models for forecasting future returns. They 'make money the old-fashioned way,' which is apparently not just by reacting to changes in fundamental economic factors.

GOOD TAXES

No less a market participant than George Soros insisted that, regardless of the length of time horizons, "market valuations are always distorted" and "the distortions can affect the underlying values" (Soros 1994, p.49).

While some opponents, e.g., Kupiec (1995, pp.102-103) argued that a transaction tax would create a "lock-in effect" such that investors might actually fail to "rebalance their portfolios when faced with new information", it seems to me that this sort of objection to Summers and Summers begs the question at issue. If the latter authors were right in their suggestion that "a horizon of hours" does not permit the provision of much socially-beneficial information, then some locking in would be socially advantageous from the point of view of a market's information efficiency. Of course, insofar as Soros was right, a market's information efficiency is largely theoretical rather than real anyway.

Dooley (1996, p.92) raised a more serious objection when he wrote that

> while transaction costs discourage short holding periods, it is not clear that short holding periods are associated with desirable (fundamental) or undesirable (speculative) investment objectives. Housing and land markets are characterized by high transaction costs but seem no less volatile than markets with low transaction costs. ...The assumption that speculation, or investment, based on fundamentals is associated with long holding periods is...suspect. The image of direct investment as factories that are difficult to move from country to country or a long-term bond that is held to maturity seems to provide the intuition behind the association between motives and holding periods.
>
> In fact, direct investors are not constrained by the nature of their assets in quickly responding to changes in market conditions. Since factories are clearly difficult to move and since returns to physical assets depend on economic and political conditions in the host country, direct investors can and do hedge this exposure. The most obvious hedge is borrowing from local credit markets. If a direct investor must exit a country quickly, she simply leaves the factory and the local bank loan behind. ...Direct investment may be special for many reasons—an example is technology transfer—but direct investors are not passive investors that ignore the market and focus on long-run fundamentals. To the contrary, they are often the better informed and more enthusiastic participants in capital markets.

Arguments in Favour of Taxing Financial Transactions

Similarly, speaking of horizons, Scholes (1990, pp.52-53) remarked,

> Short-term trading might not affect investment horizons. ...In
> Japan, where there has been a transaction tax on securities
> trading as high as .55% prior to April 1989 (now .3%), the
> turnover rates are even greater than in the US. In 1988, the
> turnover rate was 98%; in 1987, 96%; and in 1986, 75%.
> Japan has been championed as a country with long-term
> investment horizons, and yet short-term trading activity is
> quite high in Japan.

A turnover rate is defined as "the ratio of the market value of trades
during a specified period (usually one year) to the average market
value of all of the assets over the same period" (Joint Committee on
Taxation 1990, p.11). For stocks traded on the New York Stock
Exchange, the turnover rate for 1988 was 56%, for 1987 it was 73%
and for 1986, 64% (Scholes 1990, p.52).

Brockway (1987, p.3) suggested that some people seem to think
that any reduction in any kind of trading signals might be harmful,
but Stiglitz (1989, p.107) claimed that "prices in the stock market play
no basic informational role in the economy". With customary direct-
ness, Stiglitz (1989, pp.107-108) wrote:

> The fundamental question can be put simply: does one real-
> ly believe that the managers of GM or Ford base their deci-
> sions about whether or how to invest on the prices that they
> see on the stock market? Do they think that those prices—
> reflecting judgments of the dentists in Peoria and the retired
> insurance salesmen in Florida—have much, if anything, to
> add to the analysis of their own market research depart-
> ments and the reports from their engineers concerning costs
> of various projects? Any manager who argued that *because*
> the price of his stock was high it was therefore a good idea
> to invest more would, I suspect, quickly find himself looking
> for another job. ...managers do not glean information about
> what machines to buy or where to build a new plant—the
> information they need for making intelligent investment
> decisions—from looking at market prices. The fact that stock
> market prices and investment decisions may be correlated
> may simply reflect the fact that managers and the market
> are responding to some of the same signals concerning the
> firm's prospects.

Responding to Stiglitz's view of GM and Ford managers, Ross (1989,
p.118) claimed that "Those of us who know such managers find it difficult to imagine a topic of greater concern to them: it is simply the

height of *naïveté* to imagine otherwise". It seems to me that these two authors are partly right and partly wrong. Stiglitz is right about the fact that there is in general no logical connection between stock market prices and particular machines and plant locations. For example, if the price of Ford stock increased dramatically, that would not necessarily imply anything about the purchase of any particular new machine or the location of any new plant. On the other hand, if the price of Ford Stock decreased dramatically, any plans in the works for new purchases or locations might reasonably be put on hold. Clearly, both authors agree that there is a correlation between market prices and investment decisions. They seem to disagree only about how such knowledge is typically used, and that may be the result of an asymmetry in its usefulness.

15. Besides encouraging managers to focus on relatively long-term investments, "transaction taxes that tie shareholders to firms may induce shareholders to take a more active role in monitoring management, and insuring that proper planning and investment activities take place" (Summers and Summers 1990, p.166; Stiglitz 1989, p.109). The hope is that with more long-term investments, shareholders would have the opportunity and would be encouraged to become more familiar with the long-term performance of managers and companies in their portfolios. The result would be greater attention paid to industrial innovation and development rather than merely to quarterly gains in stock prices or profits from quick turnovers.

16. A Tobin tax would help arrest another socially disadvantageous aspect of securities trading versus the financing of real investment, namely, engaging in zero sum games with questionable social benefits. Assuming that capital markets serve some socially useful purposes in promoting international investments and that such markets would probably be significantly reduced if all speculative trading was eliminated, it would be a mistake to argue that because such trading can be characterized directly as zero sum, it is therefore also indirectly and totally zero sum. In the same way that a group might get pleasure and other more material benefits from watching two chess players play out a zero sum game, society and the international financial system as a whole might and no doubt do enjoy some benefits from the activities of speculative traders. Nevertheless, those who have recognized the relative differences in the private and social payoffs from speculative trading have called our attention to an important feature of such trading. A good review of differences between the so-called "pie-slicers" or "asset-rearrangers" on the one hand versus "pie enlargers" or "asset enlargers" on the other hand may be found in Hardin (1991), going back to the nineteenth century. For example, Summers and Summers (1990, p.164) put the problem as follows.

> While well-functioning securities markets produce risk-sharing and capital allocation toward high-value uses, it is true that speculative trading is a zero sum game in terms of direct effects. If A buys a stock from B because A has a good tip or good information of his own—or even a particularly trenchant analysis of his own—and the stock subsequently rises sharply, A has won a zero sum game. A's gain from trading is exactly matched by B's loss. Individuals each gain from acquiring information and trading on it, but much of the gains are at the expense of others. The social gains are much less than the private gains.

And Stiglitz (1989, p.103) illustrated the point as follows.

> Assume that as a result of some new information, there will be a large revaluation of some security, say from $10 to $50. Assume that that information will be announced tomorrow in the newspaper. What is the *private* versus *social* return to an individual obtaining the information today? Assume the firm will take no action on the basis of the information—certainly not as a result of knowing the information a day earlier. There is really no social return to the information; production, in every state of nature, in every contingency, is precisely what it would have been had the information not been available. But an individual can buy the stock today, at $10, and make a $40 capital gain. He or she can obtain a four-fold return on his or her investment. Of course, someone else would have obtained the return had he or she not purchased it. The information has only affected who gets to get the return. It does not affect the magnitude of the return. To use the textbook homily, it affects how the pie is divided, but it does not affect the size of the pie.

Stiglitz went on to say that Stiglitz and Weiss (1988) were able to demonstrate that under certain conditions "many of the financial innovations (more rapid recording of transactions) that have occurred in the last decade" actually make everyone worse off. Additional examples along these lines may be found in Stiglitz (1993) and Hakkio (1994).

17. "Since the transactions tax [i.e., a Tobin tax] increases the cost of capital worldwide, it is tantamount to a surrogate tax on capital income. It could thus compensate for tax revenue lost through evasion as it becomes increasingly more difficult to tax capital under national personal and corporate income taxes" (Spahn 1995, p.5). Reinhart (1991) presents a model in which a transactions tax functions as such a surrogate tax.

GOOD TAXES

18. "The principal benefit of the adoption of the FTT [i.e., broad-based financial transactions tax] proposal to Canadians and the Canadian economy would be that it would result in an almost immediate very significant reduction in the price of almost every type of goods and services which at present are subject to consumption taxes. It would significantly reduce the actual cost of living of all but the wealthiest Canadians and those whose consumption and lifestyle are much above that of the great majority of us" (Biddell 1996, p.87).

19. If it is true that in Canada a great deal of economic activity has gone underground in order to resist the GST, then the replacement of this hated tax with a financial transactions tax might be followed by the recovery of some of this underground activity (Biddell 1996, p.91). That would be an improvement for the economy and democracy.

Arguments Against
Taxing Financial Transactions

or each of the following 20 arguments against some sort of financial transactions taxes, replies are offered that I believe are sufficient to totally destroy or seriously undermine their credibility. The first three arguments against a Tobin tax concern possibilities for evasion, and regarding all such possibilities, I think the remark by Kaul, Grunberg and Haq (1996, p.7) is a good place to begin. "All taxes", they wrote, "–income, value-added, property and inheritance–suffer some evasion, but this has never been a reason not to have them."

1. The most frequently mentioned objection to a Tobin tax concerns shifting to other jurisdictions. Briefly, as one of the strongest proponents of the tax put it, "...speculators would use off-shore tax havens to evade the tax" (Ecumenical Coalition for Economic Justice 1995, p.6). See also Green (1990) p.3, Garber and Taylor (1995) p.174, Kenen (1995) pp.188-189, Folkerts-Landau and Ito (1995) pp.96, 99 and Mackenzie (1996/1997) pp.24-25. According to Eichengreen and Wyplosz (1996, p.36), "Other than the treaties binding the members of the European Union, there is no compulsory tax treaty under whose provisions governments could be compelled to adopt the Tobin tax".

Replies: (1) As indicated above, in Eichengreen, Tobin and Wyplosz (1995), it is explicitly asserted that the tax "would have to apply to all jurisdictions".

(2) Nevertheless, it should be remembered that there are many more countries without than with any sort of financial transactions tax, and the latter still maintain robust financial markets. "Similarly," Kelly (1993, p.19) remarked, "Germany's system of minimum reserve requirements can make banks in Germany more expensive to use than those abroad, yet not all business is driven away from Frankfurt, which remains an important trading centre." As in the case of wealth taxes, the fact that most countries do not have them has not driven the wealth out of those countries that do have them (Michalos 1988).

(3) In the interest of bringing about at least nearly universal agreement, others have suggested that "...governments could tell financial institutions that any transfers to offshore tax havens such as the Cayman Islands would themselves be subject to the tax, as though they were foreign currency transactions" (Ecumenical Coalition for Economic Justice 1995, p.6).

(4) This problem could also be addressed by making "...collection of the tax...a condition for membership in the IMF" (Ecumenical Coalition for Economic Justice 1995, p.6; Tobin 1995, p.9 and 1996, p.xiv).

(5) It has also been suggested that "small countries [could] be allowed to keep all the revenues raised by the tax within their territories" (Ecumenical Coalition for Economic Justice 1995, p.6; Tobin in the Canadian Centre for Policy Alternatives 1995, p.8; Tobin 1996, pp.xiv-xv).

(6) Again, "...in order to assure compliance the G-7 nations should apply the tax to all transactions carried out by residents of their countries regardless of where the transaction is carried out", and

(7) "They should also make the chief financial officers of their corporations, banks and investment funds personally liable for evasion" (Ecumenical Coalition for Economic Justice 1995, p.7).

(8) Felix (1995, p.43) claimed that because "physically relocating FOREX dealing to an offshore haven, as distinct from merely booking at an offshore office transactions developed at home, is an expensive, high risk operation", there would probably be less of this sort of evasion than one might at first imagine. Similarly, Tobin (1995, pp.8-9) claimed that "There are considerable costs, both fixed and operating, involved in such relocations. Otherwise low wages and rent would already have offered opportunities for saving brokerage costs and existing taxes and attracted many more financial activities, markets and institutions than they have". He took a similar line in Tobin (1978, p.159).

(9) Kenen (1996, pp.111-115) provided more detailed accounts of the differences between dealing sites (where dealers are physically located) versus booking sites (where deals are recorded), and between tax collection on a national basis (when the head office of each bank collects foreign currency exchange transaction data from its divisions in all dealing sites and the grand total is taxed by the country containing the head office) versus collection on a market basis (when transactions at each dealing site are taxed by the country containing the site, i.e., the host country). Then he recommended, first, that "transactions should be taxed at dealing sites rather than at booking sites"(p.112), and second, he recommended collection on a market basis because

> If the tax were levied on a market basis, the risk of migration would grow, because banks could avoid the tax completely by establishing dealing sites in tax-free locations. But govern-

ments would have less of an incentive to offer such tax havens. A country can benefit indirectly by luring foreign banks to its foreign exchange market: jobs are created, buildings are erected and property values will rise. But it cannot confer a competitive advantage on its own banks simply by refusing to impose the tax. Moreover, for a country like Singapore, which has a large local market, the revenues accruing from the tax may exceed those obtainable from trying to attract additional tax-free business (p.114).

(10) Since about "80% of global FOREX trading is carried out in seven financial center countries, ...An agreement among the seven on a uniform Tobin tax would suffice to keep the offshore relocation threat a relatively distant one" (Felix 1995, p.43; Tobin 1996, p.xiv).

(11) Another factor reducing the scope of required regulatory arrangements is the fact that nearly three quarters of global spot transactions tend to be inter-dealer exchanges, "mainly chains of inter-bank transactions that are set off as banks readjust their FOREX inventories" (Felix 1995, p.56). Clearly, the relatively small numbers of significant players implies that relatively small numbers of regulating authorities would be required to ensure acceptable levels of compliance.

(12) Besides, "Attempts by rogue traders to evade the tax illegally can be expected, but large trading institutions are not likely to risk reputation in order to evade a small tax. They can be expected to push against the legal limits through financial innovating, but not blatantly violate them" (Felix 1995, p.43). In any case, Frankel (1996, p.67) thought that the world "could withstand a few 'outlaw' states like North Korea and Iraq, since they are already so cut off from international financial business".

(13) From Walker's (1993, p.9) point of view, because

> The more than $900 billion traded on the world's currency exchanges every day is recorded and most of the transactions are accomplished on the world's most sophisticated data network, [the transactions are]...at least in theory, easily taxable. ...Technically, such a tax would be remarkably easy to collect through the computer systems that record each trade. It would require every bank and finance house active in the global currency markets (and they are already regulated and licensed) to open a separate U.N. bank account to which the tax would automatically be transferred when each new transaction is made. A levy of 0.001 per cent on each transaction would tick off $10 from every transfer of $1 million.

Spahn (1995, p.28) agreed with the previous three points and concluded, "Once the tax policy questions have been resolved, in particular the definition of the tax base, the Tobin tax is comparatively easy to administer".

GOOD TAXES

The organization of financial markets and the need for trades to be confirmed by official exchange clearinghouses (e.g., the Chicago Board of Trade) lends additional support to Spahn's and Walker's views of the relative ease of tax collection (Walmsley 1992, pp.263-267). Similarly, the birth of the Globex electronic trading system in 1992 with its membership requirements and improved market surveillance as a result of "a cleaner and clearer audit trail" will certainly facilitate routine taxation once the political hurdles are cleared (Powers 1993, pp.12-14). Indeed, if Powers is right,

> Globex, the electronic exchange joint venture between the CME [Chicago Mercantile Exchange] and CBOT [Chicago Board of Trade]..., is representative of the next generation of exchanges and worldwide markets. Such markets will utilize the technology of communications and the advances in international legal theory to conduct trading, pricing, and title transfer" (Powers 1993, p.318).

The shape of things to come can also be extrapolated from recommendations for greater surveillance of electronic money movements that have been made by the following: the G-7 Financial Action Task Force in 1990, the US Federal Deposit Insurance Corporation Improvement Act of 1991which "required the FDIC to study the costs and feasibility of tracking every bank deposit in the United States", the European Financial Crimes Enforcement Network's 1990 proposal for a deposit tracking system to "track deposits to, or withdrawals from, US bank accounts", and the Society for Worldwide Interbank Financial Telecommunication who have required since 1993 users of its messaging system to "include a purpose of payment in all messages, as well as payers, payees, and intermediaries" (Grabbe 1996, pp.71-78).

(14) Biddell and Grant (1994, p.3) recommended that the Canadian government should implement a Tobin tax on its own. Responding to the charge that such a tax "will drive Canadian financial transactions offshore", they claimed,

> most Canadian dollar transactions include a Canadian resident person, corporation, or a Canadian bank at one end of the transaction or the other. Therefore, if the tax was applied to all trades of Canadian residents, whether carried out domestically or offshore, the resident would be required to report the trade and remit the tax. Yes there will be opportunities for tax evasion, and it would be best if the tax was implemented at an international level. However, this should not be used as an excuse for not implementing such a tax here. If anything, Canada should play a lead role in the development and implementation of such a tax.

Arguments Against Taxing Financial Transactions

In contrast to this fairly bold move, my recommendation is to lobby nationally in Canada and the United States for a broad-based financial transactions excise tax and to lobby internationally for a Tobin tax. (15) In the penultimate section of their paper, Summers and Summers (1990, p.179) addressed the question, "Is it too late?". In their view,

> It may be clear that the tax is feasible from its implementation in other countries, but the trend toward abolishing transfer taxes must be acknowledged. ...In 1986, the transfer tax rate was reduced [in Britain].... Japan also reduced its transfer tax rate [in 1986]. ...To some extent, then, the imposition of a US transfer tax at this time might be viewed as bucking the world trend. However, it is quite possible that the introduction of such a tax here could affect the actions of other countries. The issues that create support for a STET in the United States—revenue needs and concern with excessive speculation—are crucial to other major financial center nations as well: a harmonized system among these countries could reduce the potential for the offshore flight of trading activities significantly, could reduce market competition, and could provide a source of revenue that is easily administered. If a STET were imposed in New York, there is at least the prospect that the rush to reduce taxes in other financial centers would be slowed or reversed.

(16) In their Online discussion of these issues, Summers and Summers (1990a, p.170) added that attempts to avoid a STET by moving offshore could be dealt with the way capital gains tax evasion is dealt with in the United States or through a register with toll charges as in the United Kingdom. These options were also supported by Kaul, Grunberg and Haq (1996, p.7). Summers and Summers also noted that the countries that were reducing their taxes were doing so in order to become more competitive with the United States. So the adoption of a STET at home would probably help sustain STETs abroad. This is a good response to opponents such as Hakkio (1994, p.27) who ask: "If the tax is such a good idea, why are many countries reducing or eliminating their taxes?".

(17) Recalling the special toll charges and Kenen's suggestion to levy the tax "at twice the standard rate on transactions with tax havens", Eichengreen (1996, p.277) added that "one partner [to a deal] will not have an incentive to shift his or her business to the haven unless the other does so at the same time. Indeed, a substantial number of banks and other traders will have to migrate simultaneously to provide the liquidity and scale economies enjoyed by the principal centres for foreign exchange trading".

2. Another frequently mentioned objection to a Tobin tax concerns shifting to other financial instruments or assets; e.g., Folkerts-Landau and Ito (1995, p.96,98,99) and Stotsky (1996, p.29). As indicat-

ed in my introduction, it is this particular possibility that draws investigations of Tobin taxes into broader discussions of financial transactions taxes in general. Garber and Taylor (1995, pp.178-179) explain the problem very well as follows.

> Suppose now that all major financial centres cooperate with the implementation of a restrictive foreign exchange policy. ...What is of interest in this context is the nature of the substitutes to foreign exchange activity in the major financial centres that would arise. ...we assume that the reach of the G-10 supervisors is comprehensive - all elements in a bank's corporate structure including offshore subsidiaries are within the web of national regulations. We also assume that every country in the G-10 imposes the same regulations on foreign exchange. [The G-10 countries consist of the United States, Japan, Germany, France, Italy, the United Kingdom, Canada, the Netherlands, Sweden, and Belgium.] ...If foreign exchange is defined as an exchange of one bank deposit for another in a different currency, gross trading in these claims will be effectively eliminated in favour of T-bill swaps in currencies with liquid (same day) T-bill markets. The swapped T-bills will be immediately sold for deposits. The foreign exchange market will shift to this form, no tax will be paid, and position taking will be unaffected. If supervisors have the sophistication to see through this subterfuge and begin taxing T-bill transactions, other methods can be employed. For example, certain combinations of stock market baskets and index options are equivalent to cash according to options pricing theory. Such combinations in one country can be swapped for similar combinations in another country - this is a foreign exchange equivalent. Again, to control this operation, the tax would have to be extended out of straight foreign exchange to transactions in an ever-widening ring of securities and derivatives markets. Note, however, that as they move away from bank deposits, such subterfuges deal in ever less liquid markets that are not perfect substitutes for foreign exchange. A point will be reached, therefore, when extending the tax to transactions in additional securities markets will cause explicit foreign exchange transaction to reemerge, although on a reduced scale. ...[The point is]...where the liquidity premium on the less liquid asset is just equal to the transactions tax.

Folkerts-Landau and Ito (1995, p.99) and Hubbard (1993, pp.10-13) also endorse this sort of objection. According to Grabbe (1996, p.13), a good example of instrument switching occurred when eurobonds denominated in dollars were issued in London in order to avoid the 1963 US Interest Equalization Tax on American purchases of foreign securities. Because the bonds were issued in a foreign capital market, they were not subject to the tax. Grabbe (1996, p.78) also claimed that "because of increased politicization of the banking system" there was a general increase in "disintermediation of funds out of the regulated banking system and into nonregulated channels", and he provided the following quotation from a 1994 US Department of State report.

> During the past two years, analysts saw an increasing use of nonbank financial institutions, expecially exchange houses, check cashing services, credit unions, and instruments such as postal money orders, cashiers checks, and certificates of deposit ... with transactions occurring in an ever longer list of countries and territories.

Replies: (1) Kenen (1996, p.119) replied directly to Garber and Taylor's argument as follows.

> ... consider the costs and risks of this [T-bill] swap. There are four extra transactions, each with its own cost, because both parties must buy Treasury bills, swap them and then sell them. If the transactions cannot be perfectly synchronized, moreover, both parties will be exposed to the risk of an interest rate change in one or both countries involved. That interest rate risk could be hedged–the two banks could agree to repurchase the Treasury bills at the prices prevailing just before the swap. In that case, however, governments could readily rule that the swap was designed expressly for tax avoidance and could thus treat it as a taxable transaction. More strenuous efforts might be made to disguise it, but they would add new costs or risks, or, as Garber and Taylor note, call for the use of derivative instruments having less and less liquid markets. All this to avoid a fairly low tax on a simple, low-risk transaction in the spot foreign exchange market!

Although Kenen provided this persuasive reply to Garber and Taylor's argument, he also provided good reasons for accepting the view that a Tobin tax could not be limited to spot transactions. Again, I can do no better than quote him.

> Clearly, a tax on spot transactions could be avoided easily by using short-dated forward transactions. A three-day forward contract is indeed a very close substitute for a two-day spot contract. A firm needing a currency on Friday would have merely to buy it forward on Tuesday, rather than buy it spot on Wednesday. Therefore, a tax on spot transactions must also be levied on forward transactions.
>   What, then, should be done about swap transactions? A swap transaction combines a spot with an offsetting forward. ...It may therefore be most sensible to treat a swap as a single transaction and tax it only once.

GOOD TAXES

>If forward contracts are taxed, futures contracts should perhaps be taxed, although the two are not perfect substitutes. ...
>If forwards and futures are taxed, should options be taxed too? ...it would be hard to justify a tax on futures if options were not taxed. The two are fairly close substitutes, and strong objections are raised whenever someone proposes a change in the trading regime for futures or options without proposing an equivalent change in the other regime (Kenen 1996, pp.117-118) .

This reasoning was sufficient to persuade Tobin (1996, p.xv). "Thanks to Peter Kenen," he wrote, "I see that forwards and swaps are so much like spots that they also must be subject to the tax. For simplicity, the spot contents of such contracts could be taxed all at once." Kelly (1993, pp.23-26) took a similar line, claiming,

>The control of derivatives is essential to any attempt to regulate the foreign exchange market. Derivatives' trading is systematically unstable and a key element in precipitating crises in the post-financial deregulation global market. ...The 1987 stock market crash in the United States vividly exposed the fallacy that the cash market and the buying and selling of derivatives were mutually independent. It also showed that apparently high levels of liquidity are insufficient when all the buyers or sellers appear on the same side of the market. ...The US experience shows that the market in derivatives and that in the underlying instrument (in the US case, stocks) are inextricably linked. The explosion of currency derivatives in the second half of the 1980s means that future currency crises could be precipitated, not in the cash market, but in the derivatives market.

Presumably, the Independent Commission on Population and Quality of Life, Dornbusch, and Biddell and Grant also would be sympathetic to these views.

(2) Regarding the suggestion that there might be an endless game of creating new instruments to avoid the tax, Tobin (1996, pp.xv-xvi) claimed,

>...I am consoled by the likelihood that these exchanges can be transformed into exchanges of liquid means of payment only at costs that would probably be no less than the tax itself. If Professor Garber would like to trade his home in Providence for an Oxford don's abode for an academic year, I wouldn't cry over the loss of the tax revenue that would have been collected, had the equivalent trade involved two opposite dollar-sterling conversions. I don't think such barters would become routine speculations or hedges.

(3) Although Eichengreen, Tobin and Wyplosz did not directly address this issue in their 1995 public forum article, I suspect that the following excerpt provides a clue to the sort of response they might make.

> The other contributors to this symposium offer compelling reasons to hesitate before throwing sand in the wheels of international finance. We have considerable sympathy for their arguments. But the task of economics is to weigh alternatives. It is not enough to point to the administrative difficulties of intervening in the operation of markets or to risks of evasion. These costs must be weighed against those of alternative courses of action, including doing nothing. ...For the world as a whole, the costs of the status quo are high if macroeconomic policy is hamstrung and if it is diverted from more fundamental targets by exchange rate swings. ...if pegged exchange rates between distinct national currencies are infeasible in today's world of high capital mobility, as we have argued, then exchange rate fluctuations are here to stay. Institutional innovation is then needed to reduce exchange rate instability and assure a modicum of national monetary autonomy. The theory of the second best reminds us that when other markets, in this case the markets for labour and commodities, adjust imperfectly to shocks, welfare can be improved by throwing sand in the wheels of international finance" (1995, pp. 170-171).

(4) Besides such general appeals to pragmatism and the specific replies offered by Kenen and Tobin, I would remind the critics that given the hypothesized sort of comprehensive agreement among the most powerful countries in the world that dangerously rampant capital mobility cannot be tolerated, it would be difficult for rogue speculators to hop blithely from one financial instrument to another.

(5) Apart from any real or threatened sanctions, there would be significant operational costs to anyone inclined to enter into and sustain the game of keeping ahead of an international community determined to lengthen the turn-around time of foreign currency exchange transactions with a Tobin tax. Grundfest and Shoven (1991, p.424) remarked that "The escalatory cycle of regulation-inducing innovation that gives rise to further regulation and innovation is all too familiar to tax practitioners and is likely to be a particularly severe problem in connection with a STET". Again, however, the fact that over two dozen countries routinely collect such taxes suggests that there is no "particularly severe problem" or, whatever problem there is, the benefits of solving it typically outweigh the costs.

(6) Given the relatively small number of financial centres and licensed dealers, the costs of surveillance are relatively small compared to the potential benefits for ensuring compliance.

(7) It is possible to design legislation that would make instrument-hopping in the interest of avoiding a Tobin tax a serious offence and that would make agents of such hopping personally liable for their actions.

3. Besides shifts to other jurisdictions and instruments, critics have suggested that there would be shifts from banks and other financial institutions to other institutions. For example, in a footnote Garber and Taylor (1995, p. 175) merely wrote: "How far the reach of the supervisors into 'other institutions' might extend is not clear. Nor is it clear how the regulation would be enforced against corporates on a daily basis". Folkerts-Landau and Ito (1995, p.99) made a similar point regarding intermediaries. "Financial intermediaries," they wrote, "pose another set of difficult problems in designing a financial transactions tax. Imposing transactions taxes on intermediaries can multiply the number of times a financial asset is taxed". Hubbard (1993, p.11) made the same point, and Spahn (1996, p.24) claimed that those who advocated a Tobin tax faced a dilemma between exempting "all financial intermediaries from the tax on the grounds that their trading is usually stabilizing" and taxing them, which would "entail efficiency costs". Shome and Stotsky (1995, pp.10-11) provided the following useful example.

> Mutual funds are an example of an intermediary where the tax could apply not only to the transactions of investors with a particular fund, but also to the transactions of the fund in buying or selling assets in its portfolio, thus raising the effective tax burden compared to an investor who purchased the instruments directly. While it would be possible to tax only the investor's transactions in the fund or the fund's transactions in the instruments in its portfolio to yield a better equivalence, such an approach could create opportunities for tax evasion.

Grundfest and Shoven (1991, p.430) constructed a similar scenario.

Replies: (1) Presumably the critics suppose that as the number and variety of institutions and/or intermediaries involved in currency exchanges expands for whatever reason, there would be a need for some expansion of the world's surveillance and enforcement mechanisms. This seems like a plausible assumption to me, and I suppose that the opponents and proponents of a Tobin tax would make different estimates of the likely benefits and costs of expanding these mechanisms. In the view of Eichengreen, Tobin and Wyplosz (1995, p. 169): "Clearly, no measure of the sort we describe here is ever 100% effective. But to slow down speculative activity and provide time for orderly realignments it is not necessary for it to be water-tight". State surveillance and enforcement might be short of perfect (as is virtually everything else in the world) and still be clearly reasonable in that its benefits far outweigh its costs.

(2) Regarding the specific point about multiple taxation, one must not forget that this would be the result of multiple transactions and that it is precisely such transactions that the tax is designed to decrease.

(3) The dilemma that Spahn imagined is based on the assumption that foreign currency exchange markets are efficient, which is very likely a false assumption, as will be shown below in reply #3 to the fourth argument against Tobin taxes.

(4) Kenen (1996, p.115) addressed the issue as follows.

> Retail transactions between non-banks would escape taxation unless they could be monitored and the parties made to pay the tax. ...Although these transactions are relatively small, individually and in the aggregate, compared with those involving banks, it may be important to tax them. Otherwise, non-banks would deal increasingly with each other rather than with banks, and the tax base would shrink sharply.

(5) The resolution of Shome and Stotsky's apparent dilemma regarding the taxation of mutual funds versus investors in such funds seems straightforward to me. Since both the intermediary and the private investor expect to profit from their individual transaction, both should be taxed. If the market will bear only one of these transactions, then that is the only one that should be taxed; but there is no good reason for the tax collector to give preference to either one. Presumably, the optimal solution would be to set a tax rate small enough to allow many players to stay in the game and big enough for the state to have a reasonable share too.

4. A financial transactions tax of any sort would distort market behaviour (Koenen 1990, p.6; Folkerts-Landau and Ito 1995, p.96,98,99). More specifically, for example, Brockway (1987, p.4) claimed,

> A STET may decrease the value of securities and increase the cost of capital. A STET may cause the price of a security to decline by the increased amount of taxes expected to be paid on all future transactions in that security. ...To the extent that firms desire to raise capital by issuing new securities, the decline in security prices would increase their cost of capital accordingly. The cost of capital also may be increased to the extent investors demand an increased return to compensate for any possible loss of liquidity or greater price volatility.

Green (1990, p.3), Scholes (1990, pp.51, 56), Koenen (1990, p.8), Dooley (1996, p.102) and Stotsky (1996, p.28) made similar points, while Hakkio (1994, p.18) provided the following helpful example.

> An STT [securities transaction tax] of 0.5 percent would increase transaction costs considerably, as an example from the

New York Stock Exchange (NYSE) makes clear. Commission fees for large institutions on the NYSE are about $0.13 per share, and the average bid/asked spread is about $0.25 per share.... . Therefore, transaction costs are about $0.38 per share in the absence of taxes. Applying a 0.5 percent tax to an average share price of $34.10 would increase transaction costs $0.17 per share to about $0.55, a 50 percent increase in transaction taxes (*sic*).

Replies: (1) Remember that the very first reason for initiating a financial transactions tax is to discipline a socially destructive sort of market behaviour (Frankel 1993). The latter would be "distorted" the way a cancerous growth is distorted by a surgeon's knife. Thus, Brockway (1987, p.3) wrote that "Some advocates of a STET suggest that a reduction in securities trading, especially short-term trading, would be beneficial. These persons suggest that large amounts of stock in the hands of investors with short-term investment objectives place undue pressure on corporate managers to achieve short-term results at the expense of more effective long-term strategies".

(2) According to Felix (1995), his models show that (as with successful surgery) the harmful effects of the market can be reduced with a Tobin tax while its benefits are maintained. While his models are not designed to address issues related to all sorts of financial transactions taxes, they are certainly relevant to this one important species.

(3) However, Felix also claimed that the "efficient market hypothesis" (EMH) positing "no unexploited profits" (Clinton 1988, p.358) from knowledgeable traders operating in a free market is unsubstantiated. "In this regard," he wrote, "recent empirical tests run on the various financial asset markets have been destructive of the claim of EMH to be a general description of reality. This has been especially so of tests conducted on FOREX markets, whose professional traders are found to systematically violate the precepts of EMH rationality..." (p.34). Similarly, Dooley (1996 p.86) claimed that "There is substantial evidence that foreign exchange markets do not behave as predicted by simple models of efficient markets. A large body of empirical work indicates that forward premiums are systematically biased and in fact 'predict' changes in spot exchange rates that are in the opposite direction to those actually observed". The case for this position was also made very well some years earlier in Grossman and Stiglitz (1980), LeRoy (1989), Shleifer and Summers (1990), and Stiglitz (1993). Nevertheless, in Spahn's (1995, 13) opinion, "the market-inefficiency thesis is not yet the accepted paradigm in the finance literature and it has to be considered with caution", and Kupiec (1995, p.102 claimed that "Although some evidence suggests that stock market prices are too volatile to be fundamental valuation efficient, statistical complications cloud the interpretation of results and introduce reasonable doubt about claims of market inefficiency". An earlier review essay supporting

this side of the controversy may be found in Fama (1991). As a reader of this book might have expected by now, all things considered, I found the defenders of the faith of market efficiency much less persuasive than the critics. However, Cochrane (1991, pp.482-483) may have reached the safest conclusion of all when he wrote that

> I conclude that we can agree to disagree. The evidence is at least as consistent with the view that we only require second-order corrections to efficient-market models as it is with the view that they should be abandoned in favor of fads and fashions. I and others like me whose research is still devoted to extending rational economic models to account for anomalies may, in the end, be wrong, but at least we are not pig-headed in the face of clear contradictory evidence. ...Ultimately, this is a debate over whether relatively free markets are effective institutions or whether other institutions, typically featuring government control, are more effective. The debate is not likely to end soon.

(4) Kiefer (1990, p.189) pointed out that "If the revenue is used to reduce government borrowing – which seems a reasonable assumption, since the tax would presumably be adopted as part of a deficit reduction package – the net effect of the tax would be to increase the funds available in the private capital markets and thereby decrease the cost of capital". Replying to this sort of suggestion, Hubbard (1993, p.22) wrote: 'While this argument is qualitatively sensible, it is unlikely that annual revenue of (no more than) $7 billion from the tax – against a federal budget deficit [in the US] of $300 billion – would reduce interest rates by an amount sufficient to offset the increase in the cost of capital...".

(5) In Tobin's (1995, p.9) view, "Given the myriad other hurdles to real commercial and capital transactions in the world, it's hard to see how this modest tax can result in noticeable distortions. Indeed, if it yields exchange rates that better reflect long-run fundamentals, it will enhance welfare". In his luncheon talk (Canadian Centre for Policy Alternatives 1995, p.4), he went even further regarding the use of capital controls. "I just want to point out," he said, "that whatever controls there were, they didn't interfere with the vast expansion of trade and a vast freeing of trade, reductions in tariffs and non-tariff barriers, and so on, and also didn't interfere with long-term capital markets".

(6) Catt (1994, p.1) took a similar line, claiming "the banks already levy charges of this kind on various transactions and there appears to be no effect. Thus the margin between buy and sell rates for foreign exchange is typically two to three per cent yet there appears to be no shortage of flows of money into and out of the FOREX markets for short periods."

(7) In response to the question "Would this kill the goose that lays the golden egg?", Walker (1993, p.9) replied "At such a modest rate of

tax, a sudden collapse of the global currency markets is unlikely. And if the frantic daily activity on the markets were to be moderated, this might not be a bad thing".

(8) Answering the question "Why has trading in general soared as it has?", Edwards (1989, p.2) asserted that "Institutions, which currently account for 80 percent of trading on the New York Stock Exchange, now pay less than 5 cents a share in commissions, as opposed to 80 cents a share 20 years ago". Since there was still an immense amount of trading on the Exchange 20 years ago when the costs were 16 times higher than they were in 1989, it is difficult to imagine any significant change in the volume of trading in the presence of a modest transaction tax.

(9) Frankel (1996, p.64) took the view that "Perhaps the most effective way of arguing against those concerned with the distortions that a Tobin tax would create is to determine whether there are alternative methods of raising $166 billion that would be less distortionary. Such mainstays of public finance as taxing incomes or international trade are probably far more distortionary".

(10) Perhaps Summers and Summers (1990, p.167) gave the most aggressive response when they wrote: "At this late date, it is fair to throw the challenge back to the supporters of financial innovation. Trading opportunities have multiplied enormously. Whose risks have been reduced in the last 10 years? Whose access to capital has been augmented?"

(11) Regarding Hakkio's specific example, first, it should be noted that when he wrote "a 50 percent increase in transaction taxes", he presumably meant transaction *costs*. Second, the actual increase in his example would have been 45%, and third, using the 5 basis point tax rate (0.05%) assumed here, there would be only a $0.02 or 5 percent increase in transaction costs`. Following decreases in costs of a factor of 16, it is unlikely that the market cannot bear a 5% increase.

5. The tax would increase exchange rate volatility by reducing the liquidity of FOREX markets (Green 1990, p.3; Scholes 1990, p.51 Folkerts-Landau 1995, p.98).

Replies: (1) On the contrary, proponents of the tax claim that the reduction of liquidity must lead to a decrease in exchange rate volatility. Thus, for example, Summers and Summers (1990, pp.160-161) wrote

> ... measures that curb speculation can discourage investment by those whose information does not rely on fundamental values. Instead, these investors rely on judgments about the guesses of others. If they discourage such 'noise trading,' measures that curb speculation will contribute to reductions in volatility and improve the functioning of speculative markets. As Delong, Shleifer, Summers and Waldmann (1988) demon-

strate, reductions in noise trading will cause prices to fluctu-
ate less violently about fundamental values, both because
there will be less speculative pressure on prices and because
speculative pressures will be more easily offset given reduced
risks from changes in noise trader demands. ...On balance, this
suggests that there is little basis for concern that volatility
would increase if short-term trading in financial markets were
discouraged. There is, however, some basis for concluding
that taxes which discourage turnover might reduce volatility
in general and the risk of fluctuations similar to 1987 [which
lead to the October stock market crash] in particular.

Notwithstanding these remarks, Folkerts-Landau and Ito (1995, p.98)
claimed that "Empirical relationships between the volume of trading
and capital flows and market volatility are...uncertain, based on evidence from financial and real estate markets. ...Summers and Summers
1990) hypothesize that financial transactions taxes would discourage
destabilizing traders more than stabilizing traders and therefore reduce
volatility in financial markets. There is, however, little empirical evidence to support such a hypothesis". Park (1996, p.213) went even farther, claiming that "empirical studies have failed to demonstrate a relationship between transactions costs and volatility in domestic financial
markets, implying that foreign exchange transactions taxes would not
decrease the volatility of exchange rates or security prices. Examples of
this line of research include Schwert (1993), Hakkio (1994) and IMF
1995) [i.e., Shome and Stotsky 1995]".

Kiefer (1990, p.181) also argued that such taxes would have no
effect on volatility. Since institutions are the dominant traders in the
stock markets, he wrote,

and their commissions have dropped substantially over the
last 15 years, if transaction costs are a major determinant of
market volatility, then volatility should have exhibited a trend
upward or downward during this period. This is not the case,
however. Stock market volatility shows essentially no trend
either during the last 15 years or over the entire recorded history of stock market activity. There are short periods of high
volatility, such as during the 1930s and during October 1987
and October 1989, but, in general, volatility is trendless. A 0.5
percent securities transactions tax would not raise the transaction costs of institutional traders to the level that existed prior
to commission deregulation. The historical record, therefore,
does not support a claim that a transactions tax would have
an effect on volatility.

Roll (1989, p.241) examined volatility figures for 23 countries before
and after the 1987 crash, and concluded that "Transaction taxes are

inversely but insignificantly correlated with volatility across countrie
and the effect is too questionable for taxes to be used with confidenc
as an effective policy instrument".

And Ross' (1989, p.118) view seemed to be sympathetic to Kiefe
and Roll's position when he remarked,

> Whenever questions of volatility arise, advocates of excess
> volatility point to the crash of '87 with what I have come to
> regard as an unseemly fondness. The real point, however, is
> not whether that was a manifestation of excessive volatility,
> but rather what a transfer tax would have done to prevent it.
> After all, markets with transfer taxes also experienced the
> crash of '87.

Hakkio (1994, pp.22-23) made the same point and added that his analy
sis of the relationship between stock price declines and transaction ta
rates for the OECD countries two weeks before and after the Octobe
crash showed a rank order correlation of 0.03, "which is insignificantl
different from zero" (p.23).

(2) Notwithstanding all of these doubts, Stiglitz (1989, p.111) offere
some indirect empirical evidence by noticing that "Closing a marke
can be viewed as an extreme case of a prohibitive tax. [and]...Frenc
and Roll (1987) provide convincing evidence that during the period i
1968 when the market was closed on Wednesday (because of th
inability of the back rooms to keep up with the increasing volume c
trade), volatility was greatly reduced—by a factor of 1/2!"

(3) Then Umlauf (1993) offered the following direct empirical ev
dence.

> Sweden in the 1980s provides an excellent setting for a con-
> trolled laboratory-style experiment to determine just how
> taxes affect stock market behavior. Sweden began the decade
> without transaction taxes. In 1984 a 1% round-trip tax was
> imposed on equity transactions as part of a bill introducing
> taxes on a broad range of trading activities. Two years later
> the equity transaction tax rate was increased to 2%. ...Results
> indicate that volatility in Sweden did not decline during high
> tax rate regimes as Summers and Summers would predict.
> Index levels fell dramatically in response to transaction tax
> increases. ...When the 2% tax was introduced in 1986, 60% of
> the trading volume of the 11 most actively traded Swedish
> share classes migrated to London to avoid taxes. With the
> migration the volatilities of London-traded share classes fell in
> comparison with those of their companies' Stockholm-traded
> classes. ...These results thus suggest that all else being equal,
> taxes increase volatility.

Arguments Against Taxing Financial Transactions

Secondary effects of Swedish transaction taxes are worth mentioning. Capital gains tax revenues fell so much in response to lower levels of trading that transaction tax revenues were entirely offset. Trading in Swedish government debt (which was also taxed) suffered so severely that taxes on bond trading were eventually removed. The interest rate options market evaporated with the imposition of taxes.

Since the Swedish case apparently provides the clearest empirical evidence regarding a range of alleged consequences of the introduction of transaction taxes, it is worthwhile to hear the case put in the voice of its author. Opponents of transaction taxes frequently cite this case and accept its author's conclusions; e.g., Hakkio (1994, p.23). So, it is also worthwhile to mention a couple features of the experiment that make the evidence more ambiguous than the quotation suggests. The figures are from Umlauf (1993, p.230, Table 1). First, it must be noted that total revenues from the 1% round-trip tax levied in 1984 amounted to 0.82 billion SEK (Swedish Krona), which increased to 2.63 billion SEK in 1986 just before the round-trip tax rate was increased to 2%. That was a revenue increase of 221%. By 1988 the tax revenues increased to 4.01 billion SEK, for a 389% increase in revenue over four years. The total equity trading volume in 1984 was worth 71 billion SEK, doubled to 142 billion SEK in 1986 and dropped to 115 billion SEK in 1988. So the volume increased 62% in four years. In the long quotation above, we were told that "Capital gains tax revenues fell so much in response to lower levels of trading that transaction tax revenues were entirely offset." Presumably this remark applies to the whole four year period. However, it seems to me that the figures just cited suggest that the 1% round-trip tax rate was just about right, because under that regime the volume of trade doubled and there were apparently no unwanted side effects. Indeed, since the 1% round-trip tax rate was precisely the same as the rate levied in London (Roll 1989, p.235), there would have been no reason for anyone to shift their trade from Stockholm to London to avoid the tax.

Second, Umlauf's examination of the variances of daily and weekly returns showed that "The difference between the 0% and 1% tax regime variances is not statistically significant", but the difference between the 1% and 2% regime was statistically significant (p.232). The author cautiously concluded, "These statistics are...inconclusive, but they certainly do not suggest that taxes reduce volatility. ...The method used in this paper, however, is imprecise because appropriate theoretical foundations are lacking. Also, generalizing from a single data point is hazardous in discussing policy issues of such importance" (Umlauf 1993, pp.235-239).

GOOD TAXES

In Spahn's (1995, p.26) view, "such results are inconclusive for a comprehensive international tax, because—under a unilateral scheme—national traders can always move to foreign markets or into alternative tax-exempt instruments, ...which is more difficult under a comprehensive multilateral tax regime".

6. "...the proposal requires an agreement between at least the major financial center countries to levy the tax at the same rate on all private spot and forward FOREX transactions made within their jurisdictions including transactions in Eurocurrencies other than the home currency" (Felix 1995, p.40). Even beyond agreement on rates, Folkerts-Landau and Ito (1995, p.99) claimed that "For its success, the Tobin tax would require international policy coordination in tax policy, tax administration, and the sharing of the proceeds of the tax". It is unlikely that an agreement of such scope can be achieved, and therefore efforts to achieve it are probably a waste of time and other resources. Similarly Frankel (1996, pp.63-64) wrote, "Public opinion in many countries, particularly the United States, is opposed to even current levels of international cooperation, let alone to the massive increases in spending and activity envisioned in such an agenda. To assert that the needed political consensus currently exists is wishful thinking". Perhaps most discouraging of all, in his foreword to the Proceedings volume from The Bretton Woods Commission Conference of July 1994, Paul Volcker (1994, p.2) reported,

> In substantive terms, I should emphasize that considerable agreement was registered among participants with the basic propositions in the Commission Report. There was broad consensus that the work of the IMF and World Bank is essential and their assistance would be required for the foreseeable future. There was also considerable support for the proposition that the operation of the monetary system has been unsatisfactory, producing excessive volatility and prolonged misalignment at times, and that international policy coordination had been generally ineffective in addressing these deficiencies ...
> The disagreements were apparent on specific prescriptions. A number of participants endorsed the Commission's recommendation to move toward a more formal system of exchange rate coordination over time, and to give the IMF a central role in that process. Some would have moved faster. Others were quite sceptical. Interestingly, officials from Germany, Japan and the United States were clearly not prepared to support the idea, nor did they seem eager to undertake reform of the monetary system in other respects ...
> Whatever the formal mechanism, the conference discussion underscored the Commission's conclusion that the key

to improving the operation of the monetary system, and of the Fund itself, is more forceful policy direction from a handful of countries with the most important currencies.

The Commission mentioned in these remarks was convened by Volcker on behalf of the Bretton Woods Committee. Participants at the conference included a Prime Minister, 21 Cabinet ministers, 17 central bank governors, over 20 chief executive officers of private financial and industrial corporations, another 20 or so people from public financial institutions and think tanks, and "perhaps another 50 attendees at the deputy minister or vice chairman level and substantial participation by senior management and the boards of the Fund and Bank" (Volcker 1994, p.2). These are precisely the people who would have to reach some sort of consensus in order to initiate an international tax. (Some useful reviews of risk management strategies that are relatively more attractive than taxes to bankers may be found in IMF Research Department Staff 1996, 1996a, and Kodres 1996.)

Replies: (1) On this score, I think Langmore (1995, p.191) has provided the most reasonable response one could give. Granted that there are "technical and political difficulties" with proposals such as the Tobin tax, he said, "Yet the issues are quite pragmatic: does the proposed policy have greater potential net benefits for a nation or the globe than the net effect of leaving the problem unaddressed?" It is hardly asking too much for politicians to give careful consideration to such proposals and to support or reject them on the basis of their overall merits.

(2) "The question for business," he wrote, "is whether the benefits for trade and investment from reduced exchange rate volatility, reduced investment risk and improved economic policy making would be sufficient to offset the cost of paying [a Tobin tax]" (p.192).

(3) Langmore also reminded us that "...in the late 1980s the BIS [Bank of International Settlements] succeeded in achieving agreement between countries to set increased prudential reserve ratios for commercial banks. Since [a Tobin tax] would be of benefit to everyone except foreign exchange dealers and the companies for which they work, such agreement could well be possible" (p.192).

(4) Wilfried Guth (1994, p.13), a member of the Supervisory Board of the Deutsche Bank AG, optimistically made a similar point when he wrote,

> Only recently an important step in this direction was taken as GATT members agreed to establish a World Trade Organization. Just as the WTO aims at a new approach to trade policy, strengthening the Fund authority could open a new approach to improved economic policy coordination. Just as the WTO will have to closely watch relations between the

trading blocks, the IMF would be charged with overseeing the relations between the currency blocks.

Ultimately, the prime and enduring legacy of Bretton Woods is not its institutions but a belief in an international economic order based on openness, multilateralism and cooperation.

(5) Kaul, Grunberg and Haq (1996, p.8) added,

> It appears more and more likely that the national sovereignty individual countries have lost as a result of the internationalization of markets can be recaptured only through more policy coordination among states. ...All countries would thus be better off if they were to cooperate to put into place a price-based mechanism (an ad valorem tax like the Tobin tax) with a view to enhancing the manageability of national economies.

(6) More concretely, the following remarks by Griffith-Jones (1996, p.147) on international cooperation involving the British stamp tax are very instructive. "The British stamp tax", she wrote,

> does not distinguish between domestic and foreign investors. It is a tax on the transfer of legal ownership of UK shares. Transactions in some non-UK shares, mainly Australian, Irish and South African, are settled in the London Stock Exchange. The stamp duty is payable at the South African and Australian rates for South African and Australian shares, while the UK and Irish authorities share stamp duty revenues for purchases of Irish shares through UK brokers. The latter sets an interesting precedent for the Tobin tax in demonstrating that tax authorities from different countries can easily tax financial transactions involving actors of different nationalities and showing how the tax proceeds can be shared.

Addressing the practical issues of a Tobin tax more generally, Griffith-Jones (1996, p.148) explained,

> Establishing an administrative framework would be facilitated by the relatively well-structured foreign exchange market, the limited number of licenced participants and the fact that most transactions are executed by registered dealers, and that foreign exchange transactions in all relevant markets rely heavily on automated processing and on telecommunications networks. Furthermore, tax collection would be facilitated in that most relevant transactions occur in a small number of countries. ...Spahn (1995) further develops how automated process-

ing and telecommunications networks could simplify tax administration. He emphasizes that tax assessment rules could be built into existing computer algorithms. Indeed, he concludes very convincingly that, 'generally speaking, there do not seem to be major administrative problems associated with the operation of a Tobin tax, although specific difficulties
ie in detail, in particular for the derivatives markets.
n riddle relates to international cooperation and legal
nent'.

996, pp.155-154) also has worthwhile things to say about
ıula for redistributing revenue obtained from the tax.
ıean Union funds its infrastructure from a supranational
ϵ (VAT) collected by each member state, with each state
cent of the revenue it collects, no great stretch of the
uld be required to design a similar type of arrangement
Regarding a general criterion of acceptability for the for-
ed that "Defining a formula for distributing revenue that
ϵ enough to the major financial centres and equitable
:e poverty seems crucial for universal approval".
l Langmore (1996, pp.266-267) offer the following princi-
the design and implementation of a distribution formula.

ιg that agreed global tasks are adequately and appro-
funded.
ızing the overall cost-effectiveness with which the
re used.
ızing each country's relative importance as a foreign
ge market, and distributing the benefits of interna-
ction to reduce financial risk.
g equitable burden-sharing among countries, taking
ount such factors as income and population size. ...
ıing countries with low incomes and lower-middle
ddle-level incomes would retain 100% of the pro-

ıing countries in the higher-middle-income bracket
:tain 90% of the proceeds.
come countries could retain 80% of the proceeds ...
ırther refinement of the simple formula suggested
ould be to cap the contribution to be made by countries with major financial markets.

Using these guidelines, Kaul and Langmore (1996, p.267) figured a
).1% Tobin tax "would generate about $27 billion for international pur-
ɔoses".

Clearly, there are very many possible distribution formulae and this
s not the place to try to craft one that would win international accep-

tance. Spahn (1996, p.25) apparently regarded the difficulty of selecting an appropriate distribution formula as a major impediment to initiating a tax. However, it seems to me that if members of the European Union could agree to keep only 10% of the VAT in the interest of strengthening the Union, granting special exemptions for developing countries with relatively lower income levels, member countries of the IMF with relatively higher income levels should be willing to keep a roughly similar amount (i.e., 10% rather than the 80% suggested by Kaul and Langmore). Suppose, for example, we use the 1995 figures provided above by Felix and Sau (1996, p.240). Using their model, a 0.05% global tax yielded about $97 billion, with $13 billion collected by developing countries. If we assume the developing countries would be allowed to keep all the revenue they collect and the developed countries would be allowed to keep 10% of their collected revenue, that would leave about $76 billion for international purposes. Since that is still around twice the amount required to eliminate the worst forms of world poverty on an annual basis, we might allow the developed countries to keep as much as half of their collected revenue, leaving about $42 billion for international purposes. Obviously, those who negotiate the final formula should remember Griffith-Jones's basic criterion and be prepared to sweeten the pot just enough to get sufficient consensus among the major players and to provide adequate funding to eradicate poverty, and so on.

7. The implementation of a global tax would require some sort of a supranational taxation authority, and no national government would be prepared to submit to such a power. For example, the Independent Commission on Population and Quality of Life (1996, p.283) claimed that "a new international authority would have to be created to administer the substantial funds collected, to review the mechanism's operation, and to distribute the proceeds in accordance with internationally agreed priorities". Tinbergen (1994, p.88) and Kenen (1996, p.122) apparently shared this view.

Replies: (1) Although some people have recommended the establishment of some sort of a supranational authority, I think there are more people who think such a novel institution would not be required; e.g., Tobin (1996) p.xvii, Eichengreen, Tobin and Wyplosz (1995, pp.165-166), Kaul, Grunberg and Haq (1996, p.9). It seems to me that the latter group is right and that some means could be found within the IMF to coordinate the implementation of the tax around the world. Griffith-Jones (1996, pp.150-154) has provided the most constructive suggestions regarding implementation. "Even if the Tobin tax were implemented by international agreement," she wrote,

> the IMF or another international organization should still play a major coordinating and supervisory role. ...On balance,

it seems preferable to use an existing international institution because there is much resistance, especially among several major industrial governments, to creating new international public institutions. ...In addition, an established international institution is more likely to have the authority to impose and monitor the tax, and to have the financial expertise to centralize the collection and distribution of funds, particularly those used for international purposes. Because, as Kenen points out, an existing institution may want to claim too much of these resources, it would be useful to complement its operation with a small, autonomous intergovernmental global tax commission, in which, for example, proposals for distributing the tax proceeds would be made and discussed. ...More broadly, one of the IMF's central purposes is to promote international monetary cooperation–the IMF is committed to maintaining exchange rate stability and orderly exchange arrangements among its members. As the Tobin tax seeks similar objectives, it would seem appropriate for the IMF to play a role in its implementation. ...Major policy decisions (such as the determination of whether or not to establish the tax, the tax rate, how transactions with non-taxing financial centres will be taxed, broad coverage of transactions, broad use of the tax and so on) would have to be made by finance ministers or central bank governors (or their representatives) of participating governments. ...Although the rules for a Tobin tax would be set internationally, national tax administrations would assess and collect the tax.

(2) On this score, Kaul and Langmore (1996, pp.256-257) are even more optimistic. In their view,

> The tax is characterized as global because its implementation would be based on an international treaty. ...governments are likely to keep a substantial portion of the yields for domestic use–reducing budget deficits, meeting growing needs for public outlays or reducing national taxes. The major recipients of the tax proceeds would be the United Kingdom, the United States, Japan, Singapore and Hong Kong, followed by a number of industrial countries (primarily European). Industrial countries would receive about 86% of the total revenue, and developing countries about 14%. ...The Tobin tax would thus not weaken national taxation power (as some commentators have argued), but strengthen it–in some cases substantially. And since the tax would be collected nationally, governments would control the uses of its proceeds.

As indicated above, I would prefer to have relatively higher income countries retain as little as 10% of the total revenue from a Tobin tax, and would therefore not be as optimistic as Kaul and Langmore about the financial benefits for such countries. Still, these sorts of things can only be determined by international agreements, not by my or some other researcher's preferences.

8. The people who would suffer most under such a tax probably have more political clout than any other group in the world, and they are bound to offer considerable resistance. In Tobin's words (1995, p.10), "I cannot expect bankers and others who would pay the tax, or suffer any reduction it might cause in the transactions from which they profit, to approve. They, of course, have considerable influence on central bankers and on international monetary and financial officials". This view was shared by Folkerts-Landau and Ito (1995, p.99), and Dooley (1996, p.97) was even more dramatic. "My guess is," he wrote, "that the financial sector would consider efforts to avoid a transactions tax as little short of their moral and patriotic duty". Eichengreen (1996, p.283) went farther, claiming that "there is the likelihood that coalitions will form transnationally. Financial interests in one country are almost certain to ally with financial interests in another, for example".

One way to illustrate the potential clout that such people have in Canada is to review recent contributions to the federal Liberal Party. According to Cleroux (1996, p.16),

> Last year the five largest banks made an unprecedented $5 billion in profits. ...According to 1994 figures from Elections Canada, the latest year for which they are available, the banks and their investment companies were the Liberals' most generous political contributors. The four top donors to the Liberals for 1994 are four banks. The CIBC and Wood Gundy donated a total of $115,237.66, while second-place Bank of Nova Scotia and Scotia McLeod gave the Liberals $110,825.65. The Royal Bank of Canada and RBC Dominion Securities gave $89,291.79. The Toronto Dominion Bank and TD Securities gave $82,180.81.

Even if all elected Liberals were saints, which they certainly are not, they could hardly be oblivious to the wishes of people providing such material support. Besides, it is likely that many of these elected officials have precisely the same sorts of wishes that their financial supporters have.

To illustrate the potential clout that such people have in the United States, one only has to review the furore over the trial balloon that was floated regarding the introduction of a STET. According to Tax Analysts (1990, p.205),

Arguments Against Taxing Financial Transactions

Four associations that rely on the public securities market have sent a letter to budget summiteers in opposition to the securities transactions excise tax (STET) trial balloon that is hovering over the White House and the Treasury Department. According to a July 24 press release from the Public Securities Association, joined by the National Council of State Housing Agencies, the Association of Local Housing Finance Agencies, and the National Association of Home Builders, the groups say that such a tax would be materially counterproductive as a means to improve the health of the economy by reducing the federal deficit.

Lest anyone underestimates these sources, Koenen (1990, p.7) explained that

> PSA is the public securities industry's trade association, representing nearly 400 banks, brokers and associate firms in the US, UK and Japan. PSA's member firms account for 95% of the nation's municipal securities activity and include all 41 primary dealers in government securities and all major dealers in mortgage-backed securities and money market instruments.

Nagle (1990, p.144) also reported,

> A securities transactions excise tax (STET) would immediately cost 28,000 jobs in New York City, drive financial markets offshore, and likely push the national economy into a recession, warned New York City Mayor David Dinkins (D) in a September 7 speech in New York City. Joining the mayor to denounce the proposal were Rep. Charles E. Schumer, D-N.Y., City Comptroller Elizabeth Holtzman, and local business leaders. ...Schumer said that chances are 'good' that the proposal can be killed in Congress with support from Illinois legislators who represent Chicago-based commodities and futures markets. Schumer noted that other major cities with large financial industries—such as Los Angeles, Boston, and Philadelphia—might pitch in to help topple the proposed tax.

Replies: (1) I suppose the first thing one should say about such warnings is that there is hardly anything new in the fact that the relatively few powerful privileged people always have and always will resist giving up their privileges, and that the relatively many less privileged people still occasionally manage to prevail in spite of the incredible odds against them.

(2) Since I do not know how the estimated job losses in New York City following the introduction of a STET were calculated, I will not address that part of the objection. However, since I do know how some other estimates were made, I will go directly to them.

9. Writing to the Assistant Secretary for Tax Policy of the US Department of Treasury, Thompson (1990, p.17) claimed that

> According to a new study prepared by our Global Securities Research and Economics Group,... such a tax [i.e. a STET] would also have a negative effect on the economy, reducing real GNP by $25 billion, increasing unemployment by 250,000, and reducing after-tax profits by five percent. As a result, the new tax would fail to have a positive impact on the budget deficit. The slowing of the economy would reduce overall tax revenues enough to offset any revenues generated by the tax. In fact, our study suggests that, after two years, the deficit would be about $7 billion higher with the tax than without.

Similarly, Hubbard (1993, pp.14-18) offers several estimates of lost revenues based on different assumptions.

Reply: Because the whole report of the cited Group was attached to Thompson's letter and Hubbard's analyses were provided in his paper, it was possible to examine them carefully. The most remarkable thing about both of these analyses is their total neglect of any consideration of the costs of continuing with the status quo. Summers and Summers (1990, p.169) hit the nail right on the head when they wrote that "Claims that securities transactions taxes would depress the market are based on studies that take no account of the increased investor concept and the improved corporate performance that would come from reducing securities turnover". Recalling the discussion in Chapter 4 above, suppose, for example, that a mere tenth of Baker, Pollin and Schaberg's (1994) estimated $113.80 annually invested in stock trades in the United States "for every dollar raised to finance new corporate investments" was actually invested in the production of real goods. That would mean that there might be ten times the amount of investment in real wealth creation and a GDP of perhaps ten times the size of the $6 trillion figure of 1992. Granted that it is unlikely that we would see such a dramatic increase in the GDP, it is highly likely that the real growth we would see in the presence of a STET or Tobin tax would be considerably larger than $25 billion per year. Clearly, then, the self-serving, special pleading of the opponents of such taxes cannot be regarded as a serious impediment.

10. Summers and Summers (1990a, p.170) noted that opponents of such taxes claim that many of the people who would be hurt by such taxes would be "workers by reducing the return on their pension investments". According to Folkerts-Landau and Ito (1995, p.98), because institutional investors (e.g., pension plans) "hold a considerable share of financial securities", there may be less progressivity in Tobin

taxes than proponents imagine. Brockway (1987, p.2) made a similar point. Shultz (1990, p.64) claimed that in the United States about 40% of all pension assets were "private defined benefit assets", and according to the Association of Private Pension and Welfare Plans (1990, p.87), "In the defined benefit plan arena (where the employer promises a specific benefit to participants based upon a formula) the reduction in the benefit would be indirect but just as real. Because the excise tax would not relieve the employer from paying the promised benefit, the employer's ability and willingness to pay increased benefits would be diminished. In simple terms, it would cost employers more to pay the benefits prescribed by the plan. Over time, additional employer contributions would be required. Given current competitive conditions, this increased cost would be passed on to participants and beneficiaries in the form of lower benefits." In the context of a similar line of argumentation, Shome and Stotsky (1995, p.5) asserted that "In the long run,...if the financial services industry is competitive, a large part of the tax would be shifted to investors".

Replies: (1)Responding to this suggestion, Summers and Summers (1990a, p.170) claimed that "Given that most pension funds that trade actively underperform the market, a tax which discourages active trading might actually improve performance. Furthermore, for the majority of workers who are in defined-benefit pension plans, changes in pension tax rules would have no impact on the size of benefit checks". Regarding the latter point, granting that as the cost of maintaining benefits of the same size increased, there would be increasing reluctance to make any improvements, it does not follow that there would necessarily be lower benefits. Most likely there would be tougher negotiations for improvements, but we cannot know how they would turn out.

(2) More importantly, however, since it is beyond doubt that some countries which have some forms of financial transaction taxes (e.g., Sweden) also have much more generous social safety nets than some countries without such taxes (e.g., Canada), it is unlikely that the mere presence of such taxes would make any significant difference to the level of pension benefits.

(3) Apparently assuming that he was offering a point in support of this objection, Thompson (1990, p.18) asserted that "...pension funds last year accounted for about twenty-five percent of all stock transactions [in the United States], so a quarter of this tax [STET] would fall directly on workers' and retirees' benefits". On the contrary, I think that the fact that three-quarters of the tax would fall elsewhere indicates that it is fairly well directed.

(4) If a large part of the tax burden were shifted to investors, as Shome and Stotsky suggest it would be in a competitive market, then this would be evidence of the tax's Pigovian nature. Market efficiency

and consumer sovereignty are a direct function of the appropriateness of the prices and the accuracy of the price signals available to purchasers. Since ultimately it is investors who stand to profit from financial transactions, it is economically and morally right that all the costs for their activities should be covered by the prices, including the taxation costs for maintaining a healthy financial system.

11. Several problems arise concerning definitions of key concepts related to financial transactions taxes. For example, Folkerts-Landau and Ito (1995, p.96) claimed that "...it is often not clear whether certain brands of capital flows are short term or long-term. Standard balance of payments classifications, direct investment, portfolio flows, short-term flows, and others, are in general not very informative about the volatility, effective maturity, and liquidity of the flows. Indeed, the distinctiveness of these flows may be significantly less clear than these categories suggest". Similarly, Brockway (1987, pp.4-6) noted,

> Application of the STET to debt instruments as well as to stock would expand significantly the base of the STET and would remove any STET-related incentive encouraging the use of debt financing. ...[However], the line between debt and equity is not always clear; many types of stock may resemble debt and many types of debt may resemble stock. For example, redeemable preferred stock with fixed yields strongly resembles debt, and junk bonds where the risk of principal is large strongly resemble stock. ...If the STET is to apply to transfers of debt instruments, consideration must be given to defining the range of debt instruments that may be subject to the STET. For example, imposition of the STET may be limited to transfers of debt instruments that are 'securities'. For this purpose, the definition of security would have to be considered carefully. ...debt instruments that do not represent a 'long-term interest' in an entity are not considered to be securities for certain securities law purposes. ...If the STET is to be applied to transfers of debt instruments without regard to whether the instruments constitute a security, a great many transactions may be covered. Commercial loans, privately placed debt, short-term commercial paper, overnight Federal funds, passbook savings, deposits, certificates of deposit, consumer credit card charges, and a customer's deposit at a video store all conceivably might be subject to the tax. ...Selecting the transfers that are to be subject to the STET is an important element of the proposal. In addition to sales or exchanges, other possible transactions would be gifts, transfers at death, transfers pursuant to divorce, transfers to a trust, and mergers. A broad-based STET could tax issuances and redemptions, as well as any market purchases of an issuer's own stock or debt.

Garber and Taylor (1995, pp.176-178) expressed doubts about the possibility of distinguishing worthwhile hedging against potential risks from mere speculation, and Kiefer (1990, p.184) raised questions regarding definitions of 'securities', 'transactions' and 'social value'. In his view, the problem regarding 'securities' was not only that "there are numerous financial instruments with different combinations of features, but the financial community frequently creates new hybrids to serve some particular need". Presumably the interest in avoiding a new tax would create such a need. Regarding 'social value' and the idea that there might be a difference between that and the private value of a transaction, Kiefer was unconvinced. He wrote:

> Recently some analysts have argued in favor of a securities transactions tax on the grounds that it would reduce the amount of resources wasted in speculative trading in the financial markets. ...This claim, at least as advanced so far, is not based on any systematic analysis of the optimal level of speculative trading or fact finding about corporations. ...In traditional analysis, however, resources are not determined to be 'wasted' simply because they are used for an activity regarded by someone to have little 'social value'. Such a standard would be inherently judgmental. Traditionally, the amount an individual is willing to pay for an activity is regarded as the appropriate measure of the value of the activity to that person and also to society (absent externalities). If some measure other than value determined in the market is to be used as the measure of social value, it is not clear what that measure is. ...The point is, the argument that resources are wasted in the pursuit of profits in speculative activities is conjectural. (Kiefer 1990, p.190)

Replies: (1) Clearly, except for Kiefer's last quoted remarks about the definition of social value, there are plenty of issues here demanding further study. Nevertheless, it would appear that what is required are national and international agreements about basic terms and accounting procedures not unlike those that routinely occur across a wide variety of things from natural resources and agricultural products to high tech industrial artifacts and abstract intellectual property. I do not see any reason to suppose that there would be extraordinary definitional difficulties in financial matters. Following the earlier passages quoted above, Brockway (p.5) simply remarked that "Given this potentially expansive coverage, there most likely would be some carving out to do", and he proceeds to offer some constructive suggestions regarding where to begin.

(2) Regarding the alleged "conjectural" nature of the idea of social value attributed to proponents of transactions taxes, I think it is fair to

say that there is some evidence for the conjecture. At the end of the trading day there is little new real value or wealth to show compared to the enormous value of trading activity, indicating an unhealthy state of affairs. Indeed, it is ironic that people who are typically troubled by those on the political left for emphasizing the distribution of wealth at the expense of its creation, seem to be so untroubled by a similar sort of emphasis by their friends on the political right.

(3) Regarding Garber and Taylor's doubts about distinguishing hedging from speculation, it is worthwhile to note,

> The [US] Commodity Exchange Act authorizes the Commodity Futures Trading Commission to establish limits on the number of transactions and the size of the positions that any speculator can maintain or control in any futures. The Act requires that hedgers be exempt from such regulations. Because of this exemption, the CFTC must define who is a hedger and institute a procedure for granting the appropriate exemption from trading and position limits.
>
> The CFTC has established such speculative limits for many commodities (e.g., cotton, potatoes, eggs, soybeans, corn, wheat, oats, barley, and flaxseed) and for purposes of granting exemptions has defined hedging for those commodities (Powers 1993, pp.158-159).

According to Powers (1993, p.324), "virtually every other country is copying the US regulatory and legal framework for enabling, monitoring, and regulating the exchange activity". Even if one granted that it is easier to make distinctions for commodities like cotton and potatoes than for financial assets, which may or may not be true, the fact that such legislation, body of regulations, precedents, practices and so on exists must be regarded as evidence that what will be required in the financial area is not as extraordinary as some people have suggested.

(4) Kiefer was correct when he remarked that economists traditionally use a person's willingness to pay for a good or service as a measure of its value to that person, and the sum total of such payments as the measure of its value to society, in the absence of externalities. This is perhaps the single greatest defect of economics, because one's willingness to pay is a function of one's ability to pay and the latter may have little or no relation to what one needs or deserves. Since there is certainly value in satisfying people's legitimate needs and giving them their just desserts, it is a serious mistake to believe that commercial markets will somehow be able to put reasonable prices on such values when such markets are restricted by people's ability to pay. A relatively poor person may need at least as much medical care and education, and deserve at least as much justice in our courts of law as a relatively

rich person, but the difference in their ability to pay in our democratic capitalist societies implies that the former person will typically be relatively less willing than the latter person to pay. In such circumstances, to use a poor person's relative unwillingness to pay as a measure of the value of medical care, education and justice to that person is to demonstrate a severe lack of common sense and moral sensitivity. Unfortunately, that is the traditional state of much (not all) economic analysis.

12. Apart from the conceptual problems reviewed in the previous objection, there are problems related to the evaluation of derivatives, i.e., to the value of assets traded in markets "derived" from other markets. For example, Walmsley (1992, p.334) claimed that "the theory of how to value [stock] options... is a black art. It is not a science. ...there will always be room for doubt about the value of an individual option. This is because its value depends on an *estimate* of the future volatility of the underlying instrument". Spahn (1996, p.25), Stotsky (1996, p.29) and Shome and Stotsky (1995, pp.9-10) raise similar objections.

Replies: (1) One appropriate response to this objection may be found on the same page in Walmsley. Black art or science, there is enough common understanding of the appropriate ways to value derivatives to allow substantial charges to be levied when there are apparent violations of received norms. The example Walmsley gave involved the US Federal Reserve's requiring an American bank, Bankers Trust, "to take an $80 million charge to earnings because the Fed felt that Bankers Trust had not properly valued their option book".

(2) It should also be remembered that the transactions tax proposals cited earlier from both the Bush and Clinton administrations were explicitly designed to apply to derivatives in the form of options and futures. Apparently the authors of these proposals did not perceive any insuperable definitional problems.

13. Folkerts-Landau and Ito (1995, p.99) claimed that "There is no easy way to design a uniform financial transactions tax. Transactions taxes applied at a uniform rate on all financial instruments would have different effective tax rates depending on the maturities and holding period of the assets; with a single ad valorem rate, the effective burden on assets would be higher, the shorter the maturity. If assets were taxed before maturity, this would complicate the picture; a frequently traded long-term asset would face a higher tax burden than one with the same maturity held to maturity by a single investor". Spahn (1996, p.25) raised a similar point and concluded that, contrary to Tobin and other proponents of his tax, an acceptable Tobin tax would have to be variable rather than uniform. Then he envisioned another dilemma, resulting from the tax either being so high that it would destroy market efficiency or so low that it would not deter any speculation.

GOOD TAXES

Reply: (1) Apparently the feature of a Tobin tax that its proponents regard as a virtue, its opponents regard as a vice. As indicated above, one of the main advantages of a Tobin tax according to its author is precisely the fact that the tax would become increasingly burdensome as the number of exchanges of an asset increased. Hence, its uniform ad valorem rate produces appropriately weighted and thus variable effective rates. The burden of additional taxation would fall relatively more heavily on buyers than on sellers as the number of exchanges increased, but sellers would also suffer as a result of reductions in the level of activity. Tobin (1995, p.5) remarked that "A half percent tax translates into an annual rate of four percent on a three months' round trip into a foreign money market, more for shorter round trips". Since the primary aim of the tax is to reduce the volatility of currency exchange rates by reducing the number of exchanges, it is difficult for me to see this particular criticism of the tax as problematic.

(2) Spahn's perceived dilemma again seems to be based on his faulty assumption that the relevant markets are efficient and therefore any tax high enough to alter their behaviour would reduce efficiency.

14. "...a STET would represent an indirect taxation of otherwise tax-exempt state and local borrowing, since some of the cost of the STET would pass through to states and localities" (Green 1990, p.3).

Replies: (1) Given the relatively small size of the tax on individual borrowing, especially when there is relatively infrequent borrowing, and the relatively large revenues to be gained from total collective borrowing, it would be possible for the losers to be compensated somehow by the winners.

(2) Besides, because it is usually easy to find ways in which most things are indirectly taxed once one begins thinking about the reach of sales and income taxes, arguments about indirect taxation do not strike me as very persuasive.

15. According to Kiefer (1990, p.181),

> The revenue raised by a securities transactions tax would probably vary more over time than most other tax revenue sources because the securities markets are subject to substantial variation. To provide a recent example, the total dollar value of trading on the New York Stock Exchange (NYSE) increased by 36 percent in 1987, decreased by 28 percent in 1988, and rose by 14 percent in 1989. In overall terms, the 1980s have been very active times for the financial markets, both in the US and abroad. A recession, however, particularly a deep recession, could reduce both prices and trading volume significantly, thereby reducing revenues from a transactions tax.

Reply: The best way to address this problem is to make the tax as broad as possible (Stiglitz 1989). In any case, recalling the figures cited above from Baker, Pollin and Schaberg (1994), total US stock market trading accounted for only about 5 percent of the total securities trading, and the NYSE share would be some part of that 5 percent.

16. Because a transactions tax would reduce "the return on savings,... critics charge, this will reduce savings" (Stiglitz 1989, p.113).

Reply: Stiglitz's reply was that "there is little evidence of a large elasticity of supply of savings, and hence one would not have thought that a 1 percent tax would have a significant effect on funds put away for 10 or 20 years. If, however, one decided that this was a concern, one could easily allow for a phasing down of the tax rate for investments held over several years" (p.113).

17. Shome and Stotsky (1995, p.7) claimed that "a strong case can be made that short-term capital flows (and long-term capital flows) have benefits, among others, in forcing governments into credible and consistent policies". Thus, a tax on such flows would undermine the ability of markets to discipline governments.

Reply: Unfortunately, Shome and Stotsky did not try to make the "strong case". Presumably, such a case would consist of examples in which governments introduced "incredible" policies which were immediately met with massive capital outflows. I suppose such examples would not be very hard to find, for example, in Folkerts-Landau and Ito (1995), and Mathieson and Rojas-Suarez (1993).

(1) However, the fact that governments can make mistakes is not an argument against having governments, government regulation or taxation. If it were, then the fact that investors or markets in general can be mistaken would have to be accepted as a good reason to eliminate them.

(2) While Eichengreen, Rose and Wyplosz (1995, p.252) apparently endorsed the government-discipline argument, they went on to show that many "governments whose currencies are attacked do not clearly bring their exchange market difficulties on themselves through the reckless pursuit of expansionary policies. Virtuous behaviour, in other words, is no guarantee of immunity from exchange market pressures" (p.294). Thus, insofar as capital flows punish saints as well as sinners, it cannot be assumed that the impact of such flows on government practices is always beneficial.

18. Canadians, like the citizens of most countries, are already overtaxed. Even if a Tobin tax were initiated worldwide through international agreements, it would be unfair and unpopular.

Replies: (1) My educated guess is that it is true that most citizens of most countries are overtaxed compared to the privileged few who are notoriously undertaxed. Regarding Canadians and Americans, in partic-

GOOD TAXES

ular, I addressed this problem in some detail in a paper recommending an annual net wealth tax (Michalos 1988). As indicated above, part of the virtue of a Tobin tax is precisely that it would be relatively progressive (compared to, say, consumption taxes like the GST or property taxes; Ontario Fair Tax Commission 1993; Peddle 1994), and it would therefore shift the burden of taxes away from those with relatively less to those with relatively greater ability to pay. Such a shift would certainly be fair and ought to be popular. According to McQuaid (1995, pp.275-276),

> While ordinary Canadians are against paying higher taxes themselves, they do not oppose—indeed they strongly favour— higher taxes for higher-income Canadians. ...Indeed, the public's desire for higher taxes on the rich is a strong theme in Canadian opinion polling. Donna Dasko, vice-president of Environics, describes the sentiment for higher taxes on the rich as so basic as to be a 'law of polling'. "People always want higher taxes on the rich." She points to an Environics survey done after the Mulroney government's budget of April 1989. The survey, which attempted to measure how fair Canadians considered the budget's tax increases, showed that 73 per cent felt wealthy Canadians were paying too little tax while 68 per cent felt low-income Canadians were paying too much. An Angus Reid poll from April 1993 also showed that 78 per cent of Canadians supported a tax increase on large, profitable corporations. ...The public...has apparently been yearning for more taxes *for the rich* for quite a while, and saying this to anyone who bothers to ask.

(2) Regarding the situation in Canada, "In 1992, taxes in Canada were 36.5% of GDP, while in the average industrialized country they were 38.9%" (Brooks 1995, p.25). So, granting that most of us are overtaxed compared to the privileged few, Canadians are relatively undertaxed compared to the average citizens of fairly comparable countries.

(3) One must also remember that taxes are essentially prices and that, like other prices, their fairness has to be judged in relation to the value of the things purchased. "In return for their taxes," Brooks (1995 pp. 14-21) wrote, "citizens receive goods and services from government. Like prices, the only sensible question to ask about taxes is whether people are getting good value for their money. [The]...question is whether we want services such as education, health and child care to be provided through the public sector and pay for it in the form of taxes, or through the private sector and pay for it in the form of prices". Presumably, people are not simply going to stop buying things like health, education and child care services. In the worst case scenario, what may happen is that there will be a massive swing backward to a

time when women performed virtually all of the unpaid labour required to socialize, civilize and care for the young, the old and the infirm, and people went without benefits such as health care.

(4) On the issue of fairness, Walker (1993, p.9) remarked that "Insofar as the minute levy upon each foreign exchange transaction is burdensome, it is utterly fair, representing precisely the proportion that each national currency plays in the world economy".

19. Even if most Canadians and the current federal government were persuaded of the reasonableness and justice of introducing some sort of financial transactions tax, nothing would come of it because, since the beginning of Confederation, successive Finance Ministers from all parties have demonstrated a reluctance to levy taxes that are very different from American taxes (Gillespie 1991).

Replies: (1) While the history of this reluctance was admirably documented by Gillespie, it would be misleading to suggest that his conclusions were as negative as this objection implies. In fact, from the point of view of people interested in changing current federal tax policies, his conclusions were quite positive. "In summary," he wrote,

> the broad contours of revenue structure policy of the past one hundred and twenty-three years have been moulded by the following determinants, in declining order of importance – a desire for fairness, the good credit standing of the country, horizontal tax competition, vertical tax competition, the costs of administration, base elasticity, a preference for sin taxes and a minor preference for contracyclical fiscal policy. ...In short, federal governments have behaved in a manner that is consistent with the central thesis of this study – that governments, in search of electoral support, will minimize the total political costs of raising a given level of financing. ...governments have consistently adopted new tax sources, and abandoned old ones, in response to significant changes in political costs (Gillespie 1991, pp.230-234).

(2) It should also be remembered that our federal governments have shown no particular reluctance to have tax and other financial policies which are quite different from those in the United States, so long as they are favourable to their relatively privileged main constituencies. For examples, we have a Goods and Services Tax, no wealth taxes, our commercial banks have no reserve requirements and the Bank of Canada carries only 6% of government debt, while the Americans have a Minimum Corporate Income Tax, taxes on inherited wealth, their banks have reserve requirements and the US Federal Reserve carries 30% of government debt. Regarding wealth and financial transactions taxes, it seems to me that Canada is an international free rider. While Canadians whine about the possibilities of losing revenue to other

countries by driving away potential wealthy investors with taxes directed primarily at them, most other industrialized countries simply levy the taxes and, with the exception of the United States, most of them manage to provide a more generous social safety net than Canada provides.

20. Even if Canada introduced some sort of a financial transactions tax, there is little evidence that the revenue would be put to any better use than other tax revenues. Canadians have shown significant scepticism about the way their governments spend money (e.g., Michalos 1988) and there seems to be no good reason to be optimistic now. More generally, Frankel (1996, p.68) asserted that "There is no reason to think that the public sector will necessarily spend resources more efficiently than the private sector". Perhaps still more sceptically, Dooley (1996, p.102) reminded us that "Before we arm governments with another distortion and charge them to 'go forth and do good', we should carefully examine the historical record of what governments have actually gone forth and done. The record is not encouraging".

Replies: (1) I suppose there is no more or less reason today to be optimistic about the goodwill and wisdom of governments. I am usually fairly optimistic, mainly because nothing but despair follows from pessimism. On my darker days, I become very sympathetic to pessimists, but such days are generally few in number and weak in intensity compared to my brighter days. All things considered, I think one finally has to trust our limited democratic institutions and the common sense of ordinary people to muddle through to a better life with plenty of trials and errors along the way.

(2) Kaul and Langmore (1996, pp.260-261) offered characteristically practical and positive advice regarding revenues.

> Because of the modest tax rate, they wrote, the Tobin tax proceeds would generally have a small impact on recipient economies. Yet it is plausible to guess that the impact would be positive—improved national savings, the opportunity to lower interest rates and possibly employment and income expansion.
>
> Yet in order to determine more precisely the impact of tax proceeds, country-specific studies must be undertaken. The impact will vary not only depending on each country's economic and financial situation, but also depending on the amount of proceeds collected and the uses to which they are put. The impact on the UK economy would, for example, be proportionately greater than that on any other country. The addition to its revenue of about $44 billion (29 billion pounds) would be close to the UK's public sector borrowing requirement ...

Conclusion

I called this little book *Good Taxes* because I believe that financial transactions taxes in general and the Tobin tax in particular *are* good taxes. Above all, good taxes should generate enough revenue to pay for public goods and services that not only provide a social safety net for relatively underprivileged or unlucky people but also provide the resources to create sustainable human communities with a good quality of life. Good taxes should be levied roughly in proportion to people's ability to pay, and should be administratively manageable and cost effective, but these features of any tax regime must be examined in relation to the benefits mentioned in the previous sentence. In other words, in this area as in most other areas of life, one can only decide what is good or bad, right or wrong, pragmatically by carefully weighing all the likely benefits and costs involved (Michalos 1995). As I tried to explain in the work just cited, rational and moral decision making is not a logically tidy activity, but one cannot abandon such activity without abandoning one's own humanity. Accordingly, what I have tried to do here is construct a reasonable sort of benefit-cost analysis of some taxes which, I am convinced, are indeed good taxes.

It would not be useful to reproduce the 19 arguments in favour of financial transactions taxes that we have already examined in detail earlier or to revisit all the replies to the 20 arguments against such taxes. I know my analyses have left many unanswered questions. That is also true of everyone else's analyses. However, it was not my intention to provide the reader with a relatively complete description of a new tax regime which could just be accepted or rejected on its merits. We have elected officials and plenty of professional public servants whose job it is to do just that. It was my intention to persuade such people finally but many more people initially to take a very serious and careful look at the issues surrounding financial transactions taxes. For one reason or another, such a deliberate investigation has not yet occurred. What's worse, what has occurred in Canada so far has been a very constrained and confused discussion carried out in a fairly brisk fashion by opponents and proponents alike. We must get beyond this counter-productive impasse.

Concluding their critical assessment of the idea of a Tobin tax, Garber and Taylor (1995, p. 180) wrote that "We hope that the intervening discussion has made clear some of the pitfalls that await the naïve would-be regulator of the global financial markets. A policy of throwing sand in the wheels of international finance would very likely amount to little more than a futile, Canutian attempt to command the tides of international capital flows". As one "would-be regulator", I must say I found their arguments and those of other critics challenging, provocative and helpful, but not unanswerable or by any means fatal for the most recent version of a Tobin tax or financial transactions excise taxes in general. I still think and have tried to explain why I think there is more to be said in favour of than against such taxes. "The feasibility issues raised by the Tobin tax are more political than technical" (Kaul, Grunberg and Haq 1996, p.7). It will require more cooperation among the nations of the world than there is right now, but not infinitely or impossibly more. Recalling the enormous levels of cooperation required and achieved in order to address some financial crises (e.g., Mexico in 1982), it is clear that cooperative action is possible when there is sufficient motivation.

Cautious optimism was also expressed by Eichengreen and Wyplosz (1996, p.30) when they wrote,

> Identifying the effects of capital controls is notoriously difficult because the stringency of controls and other aspects of the macroeconomic environment differ over time and across countries. It is noteworthy, therefore, that all the evidence points in the same direction. Whether it derives from the history of the Bretton Woods system, the post-Bretton Woods float, the EMS [European Monetary System] or the 1995 Mexican crisis, and whether it is drawn from the experience of industrial or developing countries, the evidence suggests that restrictions on international financial transactions have had statistically significant and economically important effects. It is still difficult to leap from this conclusion to an appraisal of the likely effects and effectiveness of a foreign exchange transaction tax. But the evidence provides little support for the sceptical view.

Four years earlier, Mendez (1992, pp.279-280) wrote,

> The establishment and application of a system of international public finance is a new and potentially controversial idea, but one whose time has come. It is critically needed because the world is at an unprecedented juncture: Poverty and disease have engulfed entire nations and threaten to decimate their populations; crop failures and famines have become chronic as desertification and other forms of land degradation rampantly spread; economic and human well-being in the less-

developed countries continues to stagnate and regress even as their populations increase; and the disparities in the wealth of nations have reached an all-time high. Environmental degradation has assumed transnational and even global dimensions, threatening the oceans, the air we breathe, the world's protective ozone layer, and even safety in outer space, where our new frontiers appear to lie. The planet's resources are being consumed at a much faster rate than they are being replenished, and are threatened with exhaustion. ...

The existing international institutional pattern does not provide the concert of nations needed for solving these problems. International private finance suffers from the same kind of market failures as laissez-faire does nationally, and the limited public sector that exists internationally is oligarchic. The flow of public funds for development and welfare is almost completely voluntary, politically motivated, and patchwork in nature. It is sorely unequal to the magnitude of the task.

What is needed is a new institutional framework that can mobilize and allocate resources as governments do in nation-states. ...Although the welfare of all humankind is ultimately at stake, there are no immediate constituents. The fundamental lacuna is financial, for nations, like people, act mainly in their own self-interest. Given a choice as they now are, nations, firms, and individuals will leave it to others to take the action needed to benefit the group, especially if the group is as large as humankind. For, in a completely unfettered private economy, we all tend to be free-riders. But...in the international as well as the national arena, either everyone wins, or no one wins. The problems can be dealt with, and if they are we will all benefit; if they are not, they will continue to fester.

Taking a broader and more optimistic view, the Nobel laureate, Jan Tinbergen (1994, p.88) claimed that

> Mankind's problems can no longer be solved by national governments. ...Just as each nation has a system of income redistribution, so there should be a corresponding 'world financial policy' to be implemented by the World Bank and [a] World Central Bank. Redistribution is the core political issue of the 20th century. ...there is a strong case for much more redistribution within developing countries. But there should also be redistribution at the international level through development cooperation ... Some of these proposals are, no doubt, far-fetched and beyond the horizon of today's political possibilities. But the idealists of today often turn out to be the realists of tomorrow.

GOOD TAXES

Of course some of today's idealists are also the wackos of yesterday and tomorrow, but I think Tinbergen's remarks are still right on the mark. It is also worthwhile to recall the following passage from the Independent Commission on Population and Quality of Life (1996, p.284).

> With global wealth increasing by some $700 billion each year, the funds are there to end absolute poverty early in the twenty-first century and to conserve our planet's threatened biodiversity. The knowledge exists, together with the wherewithal. What must be added now are the will and the act. If we care enough, if we are committed enough, everything is possible.

For the past few years we have had daily reminders that we have entered the age of globalization. Although it is far from clear what that means, nobody can doubt that people living in diverse parts of the globe in the twenty-first century will be more interdependent than people have been in any previous century. Sooner or later people will realize that mindless Darwinian competitiveness must finally give way to compassionate cooperation in the common cause of a sustainable good quality of life for all the planet's inhabitants. When that time comes, it will be comforting to know that some kinds of financial transactions taxes can help provide the revenue to fund many of the initiatives and institutions that will be required in that more perfect world.

References

American Federation of Labor and Congress of Industrial Organizations: 1990, *Submitted Statement to the US Senate Committee on Finance on Taxation of Pension Fund Short-Term Gains*, Online, March 21, 90 TNT 63-39, Tax Analysts, pp.74-78.

Association of Private Pension and Welfare Plans: 1990, *Statement on S.1654, the Excessive Churning and Speculation Act, before the US Senate Committee on Finance*, Online, March 21, 90 TNT 63-40, Tax Analysts, pp.85-95.

Baker, D., R. Pollin and M. Schaberg: 1994, "Taxing the big casino", *The Nation*, May 9, pp.622-624.

Bank of Canada for Canadians Coalition: 1995, *Submission to Commons Finance Committee Pre-Budget Consultations - January 20, 1995*.

Beauchesne, E.: 1995, "Tobin tax: hit speculators, Nobel winner says", *The Ottawa Citizen*, May 30, p.C8.

Biddell, J.L.: 1993, *A Self-Reliant Future for Canada* (LNC Publications, Thornhill, Ontario).

Biddell, J.L.: 1996, *Reclaiming Canada's Sovereignty* (LNC Publications, Thornhill).

Biddell, J.L. and Jordan Grant: 1994, *Revised Proposal for a Financial Transactions Tax*. Ad hoc paper dated October 13, 1994 and provided to the author by Grant with correspondence dated March 2, 1995.

Block, F.: 1996, "Controlling global finance", *World Policy Journal*, Fall, pp.24-34.

Bloskie, C.: 1989, "An overview of different measures of government deficits and debt". *Canadian Economic Observer*, November, pp.3.1-3.20.

Bradfield, M.: 1994, "Bank of Canada should hold more federal debt", *CCPA Monitor*, 1 (4), p.10.

Brady, N.F.: 1990, *Statement of Nicholas F. Brady, Secretary of the Treasury, before the US Senate Committee on Finance*, Online, March 21, 90 TNT 63-33, Tax Analysts, pp.38-42.

Brockway, D.H.: 1987, "Memorandum on Securities Transfer Tax Issues", Online, Tax Analysts, *Tax Notes*, May 18, pp.2-11.

Brooks, N.: 1995: *Left vs Right: Why the Left is Right and the Right is Wrong* (Canadian Centre for Policy Alternatives, Ottawa).

Cameron, D.R.: 1985, "Does government cause inflation? Taxes, spending, and deficits", *The Politics of Inflation and Economic Stagnation*, ed. by L.N. Lindberg and C.S. Maier (The Brookings Institution, Washington) pp.224-279.

Canadian Centre for Policy Alternatives: 1995, *Transcript of CCPA Luncheon Seminar, Guest Speaker: James Tobin, on his proposed tax on international monetary transactions*, May 29.

Canadian Centre for Policy Alternatives, jointly with Choices: A Coalition for Social Justice: 1996, *Alternative Federal Budget 1996* (Ottawa and Winnipeg).

Catt, Allan J.L.: 1994, *Some Questions Relating to the Financial Transactions Tax*. A discussion paper on the tax proposed by the Alliance Party of New Zealand.

Cleroux, R.: 1996, "The party of corporate Canada", *The Canadian Forum*, 74(847), pp.15-18.

Clinton, K.: 1988, "Transactions costs and covered interest arbitrage: theory and evidence", *Journal of Political Economy*, **96**, pp.358-370.

Cochrane, J.H.: 1991, "Volatility tests and efficient markets", *Journal of Monetary Economics*, 27, pp.463-485.

Cohen, M.G.: 1994, *Debt and Deficit: A Problem or The Problem* (New Democratic Party of Canada, Ottawa).

DeLong, J.B., A. Shleifer, L.H. Summers and R.J. Waldmann: 1988, "The economic conse-

References

quences of noise traders", Harvard University unpublished manuscript. A later version appeared by the same authors as: "The size and incidence of the losses from noise trading", *The Journal of Finance*, 1989, **44**, pp.681-696.

De Vries, R.: 1990, "Adam Smith: managing the global capital of nations", *World Financial Markets*, July 23.

Dooley, M.P.: 1996, "The Tobin tax: good theory, weak evidence, questionable policy", *The Tobin Tax: Coping with Financial Volatility*, ed. by M. ul Haq, ACOL and I. Grunberg (Oxford University Press, New York) pp.83-106.

Dornbusch, R.: 1990, "Exchange rate economics", Current Issues in International Monetary Economics, ed. by D. Llewellyn and C. Miller (Macmillan, London) pp.13-43.

Ecumenical Coalition for Economic Justice: 1995, "Canada: caught in the currents of speculative capitalism", *Economic Justice Report*, 6(2), pp. 1-8.

Edwards, F.R.: 1989, "Prologue to conference on regulatory reform of stock and futures markets", *Regulatory Reform of Stock and Futures Markets: A Special Issue of the Journal of Financial Services Research*, ed. by F.R. Edwards (Kluwer Academic Publishers, Boston) pp.1-2.

Eichengreen, B.: 1993, "Epilogue: Three perspectives on the Bretton Woods System", *A Retrospective on the Bretton Woods System. Lessons for International Monetary Reform*, ed. by M.P. Bordo and B. Eichengreen (University of Chicago Press, Chicago) pp.193-201.

Eichengreen, B., A.K. Rose and C. Wyplosz: 1995, "Exchange market mayhem: the antecedents and aftermath of speculative attacks", Economic Policy, **21**, pp.250-312.

Eichengreen, B., A.K. Rose and C. Wyplosz: 1996, *Contagious Currency Crises*, NBER Working Paper No.5681, July, Cambridge, Massachusetts.

Eichengreen, B., J. Tobin and C. Wyplosz: 1995, "Two cases for sand in the wheels of international finance", *The Economic Journal*, **105**, pp. 162-172.

Eichengreen, B. and C. Wyplosz: 1996, "Taxing international financial transactions to enhance the operation of the international monetary system", *The Tobin Tax: Coping with Financial Volatility*, ed. by M. ul Haq, I.Kaul and I. Grunberg (Oxford University Press, New York) pp.15-39.

Fama, E.F.: 1991, "Efficient capital markets: II", *The Journal of Finance*, **46**(5), pp.1575-1617.

Felix, D.: 1994, *The Tobin Tax: Background, Issues and Prospects* (New York, United Nations Development Program).

Felix, D.: 1995, *Financial Globalization versus Free Trade: The Case for the Tobin Tax* Discussion Paper No. 108 (United Nations Conference on Trade and Development Geneva).

Felix, D.: 1996, "Statistical appendix", *The Tobin Tax: Coping with Financial Volatility*, ed by M. ul Haq, I.Kaul and I. Grunberg (Oxford University Press, New York) pp.290-300.

Felix, D.: 1996a, "On drawing general policy from recent Latin American currency crises" Working Paper #206, Department of Economics, Washington University in St. Louis.

Felix, D. and R. Sau: 1996, "On the Revenue Potential and Phasing in of the Tobin Tax" *The Tobin Tax: Coping with Financial Volatility*, ed. by M. ul Haq, I. Kaul and I Grunberg (Oxford University Press, New York) pp.223-254..

Fennell, T. and D. Thomas: 1996, "Taxing foreign havens", *Maclean's*, November 4, pp.44-45.

Folkerts-Landau, D. and T. Ito: 1995, *International Capital Markets: Developments Prospects, and Policy Issues* (International Monetary Fund, Washington).

Fortin, P.: 1996, "The Canadian fiscal problem: the macroeconomic connection" *Unnecessary Debts*, ed. by L. Osberg and P. Fortin (James Lorimer and Co., Toronto) pp.26-38.

Frankel, J.A.: 1993, *On Exchange Rates* (The MIT Press, Cambridge, Mass.).

Frankel, J.A.: 1996, "How well do foreign exchange markets work: Might a Tobin tax help?", *The Tobin Tax: Coping with Financial Volatility*, ed. by M. ul Haq, I.Kaul and I Grunberg (Oxford University Press, New York) pp.41-81.

French, K. and R. Roll: 1987, "Stock return variances: the arrival of information and the reaction of traders", *Journal of Financial Economics*, **15**, pp.5-26.

Garber, P. and M.P. Taylor: 1995, "Sand in the wheels of foreign exchange markets: a sceptical note", *The Economic Journal*, **105**, pp. 173-180.

References

Gillespie, W.I.: 1991, *Tax, Borrow and Spend: Financing Federal Spending in Canada, 1867-1990* (Carleton University Press, Ottawa).

Gillespie, W.I.: 1996, "A brief history of government borrowing in Canada", *Unnecessary Debts*, ed. by L. Osberg and P. Fortin (James Lorimer and Co., Toronto) pp.1-25.

Gilpin, R.: 1987, *The Political Economy of International Relations* (Princeton University Press, Princeton, New Jersey).

Goulder, L.H., I.W.H. Parry and D. Burtraw: 1996, *Revenue-Raising vs Other Approaches to Environmental Protection: The Critical Significance of Pre-Existing Tax Distortions*, NBER Working Paper No.5641, June, Cambridge, Massachusetts.

Grabbe, J.O.: 1996, *International Financial Markets*, third edition (Prentice-Hall, Englewood Cliffs).

Green, M.S.: 1990, "PSA warns against securities transfer excise tax", Online, July 9, 90 TNT 142-43, Tax Analysts, pp.2-4.(Full text of a letter from the Executive Vice President of the Public Securities Association to the Director of the US Office of Management and Budget.)

Greenaway, D.: 1995, "Policy forum: sand in the wheels of international finance" *The Economic Journal*, **105**, pp. 160-161.

Greider, W.: 1987, *Secrets of the Temple: How the Federal Reserve Runs the Country* (Simon and Schuster, New York).

Griffith-Jones, S.: 1996, "Institutional arrangements for a tax on international currency transactions", *The Tobin Tax: Coping with Financial Volatility*, ed. by M. ul Haq, I.Kaul and I. Grunberg (Oxford University Press, New York) pp.143-158.

Grossman, S.J. and J.E. Stiglitz: 1980, "On the impossibility of informationally efficient markets", *American Economic Review*, **70** (3), pp.393-408.

Grundfest, J.A. and J.B. Shoven: 1991, "Adverse implications of a securities transactions excise tax", *Journal of Accounting , Auditing and Finance*, 6 (4), pp.409-442.

Guth, W.: 1994, "Presentation", *Bretton Woods: Looking to the Future*, Conference Proceedings, Washington, D.C., July 20-22, 1994 (Bretton Woods Committee, Washington) pp.11-13.

Guttmann, R. (ed): 1989, *Reforming Money and Finance: Institutions and Markets in Flux* (M. E. Sharpe, Inc., Arrnonk, New York).

Hakkio, C.: 1994, "Should we throw sand in the gears of financial markets?", *Economic Review*, Federal Reserve Bank of Kansas City **79**(2), pp.17-31.

Haq, M. ul, I. Kaul and I. Grunberg (eds.): 1996, *The Tobin Tax: Coping with Financial Volatility* (Oxford University Press, New York).

Hardin, H.: 1991, *The New Bureaucracy: Waste and Folly in the Private Sector* (McClelland and Stewart, Toronto).

Helleiner, E.: 1 994, *States and the Reemergence of Global Finance. From Bretton Woods to the 1990s* (Cornell University Press, Ithaca, New York).

Hubbard, R.G.: 1993, "Securities transactions taxes: tax design, revenue and policy considerations", Online, November 22, 61 Tax Notes 985, Tax Analysts, pp.8-37.

IMF Research Department Staff: 1996, "Global financial markets: moving up the learning curve", *Finance and Development*, **33**(4), pp.19-21.

IMF Research Department Staff: 1996a, "Managing risks to the international banking system", *Finance and Development*, **33**(4), pp.26-28.

Independent Commission on Population and Quality of Life: 1996, *Caring for the Future* (Oxford University Press, New York).

International Labour Organization: 1994, *Towards Full Employment: Contribution of the ILO to the second session of the Preparatory Committee for the World Summit for Social Development* (ILO, Geneva).

Joint Committee on Taxation: 1990, *Tax Treatment of Short-Term Trading* (JCS- 8-90) Online, March 19, 90 TNT 61-12, Tax Analysts, pp.2-30.

Kaul, I.: 1995, "Beyond financing: Giving the United Nations power of the purse", *Futures*, **27**, pp.181-188.

Kaul, I., I. Grunberg and M. ul Haq: 1996, "Overview", *The Tobin Tax: Coping with Financial Volatility*, ed. by M. ul Haq, I. Kaul and I. Grunberg (Oxford University Press, New York) pp.1-12.

References

Kaul, I. and J. Langmore: 1996, "Potential uses of the revenue from a Tobin tax", *The Tobin Tax: Coping with Financial Volatility*, ed. by M. ul Haq, I. Kaul and I.Grunberg (Oxford University Press, New York) pp.255-272.

Kelly, R.: 1993, *Taxing the Speculator: the Route to FOREX Stability*, Fabian Society Discussion Paper No.15 (Fabian Society, London).

Kenen, P.B.: 1995, "Capital controls, the EMS and EMU", *The Economic Journal*, 105, pp.181-192.

Kenen, P.B.: 1996, "The feasibility of taxing foreign exchange transactions", *The Tobin Tax: Coping with Financial Volatility*, ed. by M. ul Haq, I. Kaul and I. Grunberg (Oxford University Press, New York) pp.109-128.

Keynes, J.M.: 1936, *The General Theory of Employment, Interest and Money* (Harcourt, Brace, New York).

Klein, S.: 1996, *Good Sense versus Common Sense: Canada's Debt Debate and Competing Hegemonic Projects* (Master's Thesis, Simon Fraser University, Burnaby, BC).

Kiefer, D.W.: 1990, "The security transactions tax: an overview of the issues", Online, August 13, 48 *Tax Notes* 885, Tax Analysts, pp.172-204.

Kodres, L.E.: 1996, "Foreign exchange markets: structure and systemic risks", *Finance and Development*, 33(4), pp.22-25.

Koenen, A.V.: 1990, "PSA warns securities transaction tax could harm markets", Online, August 22, 90 TNT 174-21, Tax Analysts, pp.6-9. (Full text of a letter from the Chairman of the Public Securities Association to the US Secretary of the Treasury.)

Kupiec, P.H.: 1995, "A securities transactions tax and capital market efficiency", *Contemporary Economic Policy*, 13, pp.101-112.

Langmore, J.: 1995, "Restructuring economic and financial power", *Futures*, 27, pp.189-194.

LeRoy, S.F.: 1989, "Efficient capital markets and martingales", *Journal of Economic Literature*, 27, pp.1583-1621.

Library of Parliament: 1996, "Financial transactions taxes: pros, cons, design issues and revenue estimates" (Ottawa).

Library of Parliament: 1996a, "Financial transactions taxes: the international experience and the lessons for Canada" (Ottawa).

Mackenzie, H.: 1996/1997, "FTT criticized as unrealistic and unworkable", *CCPA Monitor*, 3(6) pp.24-25.

Mathieson, D.J. and L. Rojas-Suarez: 1993, *Liberalization of the Capital Account: Experiences and Issues*, Occasional Paper 103 (International Monetary Fund, Washington, D.C.).

McCracken, M.C.: 1996, "Recent Canadian monetary policy: deficit and debt implications", *Unnecessary Debts*, ed. by L. Osberg and P. Fortin (James Lorimer and Co., Toronto) pp.71-89.

McGrath, M.A.: 1990, *Testimony before the US Senate Committee on Finance of Michael A. McGrath, Treasurer, State of Minnesota, on behalf of the National Association of State Treasurers and the Council of Institutional Investors, Washington, D.C.*, Online, March 21, 90 TNT 63-38, Tax Analysts, pp.67-71.

McQuaig, L.: 1993, *The Wealthy Banker's Wife: The Assault on Equality in Canada* (Penguin Books Canada, Toronto).

McQuaig, L.: 1995, *Shooting the Hippo: Death by Deficit and other Canadian Myths* (Penguin Books Canada, Toronto).

Mendez, R.P.: 1992, *International Public Finance: A New Perspective on Global Relations* (Oxford University Press, New York).

Mendez, R.P.: 1995, "Paying for peace and development", *Foreign Policy*, 100, pp.19-31.

Michalos, A.C.: 1988, "A case for a progressive annual net wealth tax", *Public Affairs Quarterly*, 2, pp.105-140. Reprinted in Michalos 1995.

Michalos, A.C.: 1995, *A Pragmatic Approach to Business Ethics* (Sage Pub., Thousand Oaks, California).

Michalos, A.C.: 1997, "Combining social, economic and environmental indicators to measure sustainable human development", *Social Indicators Research*, to be published.

Mimoto, H. and P. Cross: 1991, "The growth of the federal debt", *Canadian Economic Observer*, June, pp.3.1 -3.18.

Nagle, F.R.: 1990, "NYC Mayor Dinkins and Rep. Schumer blast proposed securities trans-actions tax", Online, September 17, 48 *Tax Notes* 1558, p.144.

Oates, W.E.: 1995, "Green taxes: Can we protect the environment and improve the tax sys-tem at the same time?", *Southern Economic Journal*, 61(4), pp.915-922.

Ontario Fair Tax Commission: 1993, *Fair Taxation in a Changing World: Report of the Ontario Fair Tax Commission* (University of Toronto Press, Toronto).

Peddle, F.K.: 1994, *Cities and Greed: Taxes, Inflation and Land Speculation* (Canadian Research Committee on Taxation, Ottawa).

Pope, W.H.: 1996, *All You Must Know about Economics* (Comer Publications, Toronto).

Powers, M.J.: 1993, *Starting Out in Futures Trading* (Irwin Professional Publishing, Chicago).

Public Securities Association: 1990, *Statement to the US Senate Committee on Finance on Short-Term Securities Trading*, Online, March 21, 90 TNT 63-41, Tax Analysts, pp.97-100.

Reinhart, V.: 1991, "The 'Tobin tax', asset accumulation, and the real exchange rate", *Journal of International Money and Finance*, 10(4), pp.420-431.

Rice, J.J. and M.J. Prince: 1993, "Lowering the safety net and weakening the bonds of nationhood: social policy in the Mulroney years", *How Ottawa Spends 1993-1994, A More Democratic Canada...?*, ed. by Susan D. Phillips (Carleton University Press, Ottawa) pp.381-416.

Roll, R.: 1989, "Price volatility, international market links, and their implications for regu-latory policies", *Journal of Financial Services Research*, 3, pp.211- 246.

Rosenbluth, G.: 1996, "The debt and Canada's social programs", *Unnecessary Debts*, ed. by L. Osberg and P. Fortin (James Lorimer and Co., Toronto) pp.90-111.

Ross, S.A.: 1989, "Commentary: Using tax policy to curb speculative short-term trading", *Journal of Financial Services Research*, 3, pp.117-120.

Russell, F.: 1991, "Political interference suggested by Stats Can move", *Winnipeg Free Press*, October 9, p.6

Scholes, M.S.: 1990, *Tax Treatment of Short-Term Trading*, Online, March 21, 90 TNT 63-36, Tax Analysts, pp.50-58.

Schwert, G.W.: 1993, "Stock market volatility", *Journal of Financial Service Research*, 46 (May-June), pp.23-24

Schwert, G.W. and P.J. Seguin: 1993, "Securities transactions taxes: An overview of costs, benefits and unresolved questions", *Financial Analysts Journal*, 46, pp.27-35.

Shleifer, A. and L.H. Summers: 1990, "The noise trader approach to finance", *Journal of Economic Perspectives*, 4(2), pp.19-33.

Shome, P. And J.G. Stotsky: 1995, *Financial Transactions Taxes*, IMF Fiscal Affairs Department, Working Paper 77, August, Washington, D.C.

Shultz, R.E.: 1990, *Testimony before the US Senate Committee on Finance of Robert E. Shultz, Co-Chairman of the Working Group on Taxation, Committee on Investment of Employee Benefit Assets of the Financial Executives Institute*, Online, March 21, 90 TNT 63-67, Tax Analysts, pp.60-65.

Siroonian, J.: 1993, "Investment income of Canadians", *Canadian Economic Observer*, June, pp.3.1-3.11.

Smeeding, T.M. and L. Rainwater: 1991, *Cross-National Trends in Income Poverty and Dependency: The Evidence for Young Adults in the Eighties* (Prepared for the JCPS Conference, Washington, D.C., September 20-21.

Soros, G.: 1994, *The Alchemy of Finance: Reading the Mind of the Market* (John Wiley and Sons, New York).

Spahn, P.B.: 1995, *International Financial Flows and Transactions Taxes: Survey and Options*, IMF Working Paper 60, June, Washington, D.C.

Spahn, P.B.: 1996, "The Tobin tax and exchange rate stability", *Finance and Development*, 33, pp.24-27.

Statistics Canada: 1986, *Characteristics of high income families 1980* (Minister of Supply and Services Canada, Ottawa, Cat.#13-584).

Stiglitz, J.E.: 1989, "Using tax policy to curb speculative short-term trading", *Journal of Financial Services Research*, 3, pp.101-115.

References

Stiglitz, J.E.: 1993, "The role of the state in financial markets", *Proceedings of the World Bank Annual Conference on Development Economics 1993* (The World Bank, Washington, D.C.) pp.19-52..

Stiglitz, J.E. and A. Weiss: 1988, *Banks as Social Accountants and Screening Devices for the Allocation of Credit,* NBER Working Paper No. 2710, September, Cambridge, Massachusetts.

Stotsky, J.G.: 1996, "Why a two-tier Tobin tax won't work", *Finance and Development,* 33, pp.28-29.

Summers, L.H. and V.P. Summers: 1990, "When financial markets work too well: a case for a securities transaction tax", *Innovation and Technology in the Markets: A Reordering of the World's Capital Market Systems,* ed. by D.R. Siegel (McGraw-Hill Book Co., London) pp.151-181.

Summers, L.H. and V.P. Summers: 1990a, "The case for a securities transactions excise tax", Online, August 13, 48 *Tax Notes* 879, pp.161-171.

Svensson, L.E.O.: 1994, "Fixed exchange rates as a means to price stability: What have we learned?", *European Economic Review,* 38, pp.447-468.

Tax Analysts: 1990, "Securities transactions tax opposed by housing and finance groups" Online, July 30, 48 *Tax Notes* 578, p.205.

Thompson, B.E.: 1990, "Merrill Lynch says securities transactions tax would harm the economy and add to the budget deficit", Online, August 6, 90 TNT 162-46, Tax Analysts, pp.16-21. (Full text of letter from Thompson to the Assistant Secretary for Tax Policy, US Department of Treasury.)

Tinbergen, J.: 1994, "Global governance for the 21st century", *Human Development Report 1994 (UNDP,* New York) p.88.

Tobin, J.: 1974, *The New Economics One Decade Older* (Princeton University Press Princeton).

Tobin, J.: 1978, "A proposal for international monetary reform", *The Eastern Economic Journal,* 4(3-4), pp.153-159.

Tobin, J.: 1984, "On the efficiency of the financial system", *Lloyds Bank Review,* July, pp.1-15.

Tobin, J.: 1994, "A tax on international currency transactions", *Human Development Report 1994 (UNDP,* New York) p.70.

Tobin, J.: 1995, *A Currency Transactions Tax. Why and How.* A paper presented at the Conference on Globalization of Markets, CIDEI Universita "La Sapienza", Rome October 27-28, 1994, Revised 1/11/95.

Tobin, J.: 1996, "Prologue", *The Tobin Tax: Coping with Financial Volatility,* ed. by M. ul Haq, I. Kaul and I. Grunberg (Oxford University Press, New York) pp.x-xviii.

Tornell, A.: 1990, "Real vs financial investment: Can Tobin taxes eliminate the irreversibility distortion?", *Journal of Development Economics,* 32, pp.419- 444.

Umlauf, S.R.: 1993, "Transaction taxes and the behavior of the Swedish stock market" *Journal of Financial Economics,* 22, pp.227-240.

United Nations Development Programme: 1994, *Human Development Report 1994* (UNDP, New York).

Volcker, P.A.: 1994, "Forward", *Bretton Woods: Looking to the Future,* Conference Proceedings, Washington, D.C., July 20-22, 1994 (Bretton Woods Committee Washington) pp.1-3.

Wachtel, H.M.: 1994, "Taming global money", *Beyond Bretton Woods: Alternatives to the Global Economic Order,* ed. by J. Cavanagh, D. Wysham and M. Arruda (Pluto Press London) pp.74-81.

Walker, M.: 1993, "Global taxation: paying for peace", *Orbis: A Journal of World Affairs* Fall, pp.7-12.

Walmsley, J.: 1992, *The Foreign Exchange and Money Markets Guide* (John Wiley and Sons New York).

Workman, T.: 1996, *Banking on Deception: The Discourse of Fiscal Crisis* (Fernwood Halifax).

About the Author

lex Michalos is 61, married, and has three grown children. He has four university degrees: a BA (Western Reserve U.), MA, BD and PhD (University of Chicago), and is currently teaching politics and social science at the University of Northern British Columbia in Prince George, BC, Canada. He has been a full-time university professor since 1962, spending 28 years at the University of Guelph, Ontario.

He was elected Fellow of the Royal Society of Canada in 1993 and appointed to the Science Policy Committee. In 1995 he was elected to the governing Council of Academy II (Humanities and Social Sciences) of the Society, and appointed to the Selection Committee for the McNeil Medal for the Public Awareness of Science and, the following year, to the Public Awareness of Science Committee..

In 1996 the International Society for Quality of Life Studies gave him the Quality of Life-Social Indicators Educator Award for Extraordinary Contributions to Quality of Life Research.

He has published 18 books, over 60 articles and 160 reviews, and his work has been translated into Japanese, Chinese, German, Polish, French and Spanish. Most of his scholarly work, consulting and teaching has been concerned with improving the quality of life through applications of science and technology, and improving science and technology by recognizing them as human creations whose ultimate justification lies in their capacity to improve the quality of life.

His first four books (1969-1978) involve the integration of mathematical logic and the formal theories of probability and statistics with human values to be used in practical decision-making, the application of probability theory to·the problem of determining the acceptability of scientific theories, and a general theory of rational and moral decision-making.

His five volume treatise, *North American Social Report: A Comparative Study of the Quality of Life in Canada and the USA from 1964 to 1974 (1980-82)*, received the 1984 Secretary of State's Award for Excellence in interdisciplinary studies in the area of Canadian Studies. It is the most extensive and intensive attempt to integrate the results of scientific research in sociology, economics, psychology, geography, politics and environmental science in order to provide a quantitative measure of the quality of life.

His Science for Peace volume on *Militarism and the Quality of Life* (1989) argued that some scientific research and development was counter-productive from the point of view of improving the quality of life, making it necessary for researchers first but finally for all citizens to consider ways to obtain an optimum mix of appropriate R and D.

His four-volume *Global Report on Student Well-Being* (1991-1993) gives the results of a survey of over 18,000 university students in 39 countries. It is the biggest international survey of students ever undertaken and involves the most extensive testing of a social scientific theory across national boundaries. The theory, which was invented by Michalos, is called Multiple Discrepancies Theory. It provides a new foundation for research in technology and risk assessment, micro-economics, exchange and decision theories, and moral consequentialist theories.

His published scholarly articles include studies of rational and moral decision making, values in science and in science education, values in the sociological, historical and philosophical study of science and technology, a design for a science court to adjudicate controversial public issues in technology and science, the role of facts and values in technology and risk assessment, the quantitative study of the growth and quality of science and technology, feminism and the quality of life, the taxation of wealth, business ethics, trust and the quality of life, and the impact of public goods on human migration.

His book on *A Pragmatic Approach to Business Ethics* was published in the spring of 1995.

He founded and still edits three scholarly journals, *Social Indicators Research* (an international and interdisciplinary journal for quality-of-life measurement), the *Journal of Business Ethics*, and *Teaching Business Ethics* (the latter two with Deborah Poff). He is serving or has served on the Editorial Boards of the *Journal of Medicine and Philosophy, Research on Philosophy and Technology, Theory and Decision, International Journal of Value-Based Management, Optimum* (the journal of public sector management) and the *South Asian Journal of Psychology.*

He is a past President of the International Society for Philosophy and Technology (1983-85), a past member of the Board of Governors of the Philosophy of Science Association (1978-82), and the current Chair of the Working Group on Social Indicators and Social Reporting of the International Sociological Association.

He has been a consultant to the Department of Veteran's Affairs, Department of Secretary of State, Statistics Canada, Correctional

Services of Canada, Science Council of Canada, Department of Industry, Trade and Commerce, Regional Planning Board of Hamilton-Wentworth (Ontario), Solicitor General of Nova Scotia, United Nations Educational, Scientific and Cultural Organization (UNESCO, Paris), the Organization for Economic Cooperation and Development (OECD, Paris), the Royal Commission on Electoral Reform and Party Financing, the Ontario Fair Tax Commission, the National Round Table on the Environment and the Economy, the British Columbia Commission on Resources and Environment, the Fraser Basin Management Board, Forest Renewal BC, and government agencies of Norway, Sweden, Germany, Japan, Italy, Republic of South Africa, and the United States.

Other Books from Science for Peace

(with Dundurn Press)

United Nations Reform: Looking Ahead after Fifty Years, edited by Eric Fawcett and Hanna Newcombe. 1995. 336 p.

World Security: The New Challenge, edited by Carl G. Jacobsen, Morris Miller, Metta Spencer, and Eric L. Tollefson. 1994. 282 p.

(with Samuel Stevens)

Arctic Alternatives: Civility or Militarism in the Circumpolar North, edited by Franklyn Griffiths. 1992. 313 p.

Hopes and Fears: The Human Future, edited by Hanna Newcombe. 1992. 195 p.

Unarmed Forces, edited by Graeme MacQueen. 1992. 129 p.

Disarmament's Missing Dimension: A UN Agency to Administer Multilateral Treaties, The Markland Policy Group. 1990. 150 p.

Accidental Nuclear War: Proceedings of the Eighteenth Pugwash Workshop on Nuclear Forces, edited by Derek Paul, Michael D. Intriligator, and Paul Smoker. 1990. 169 p.

Militarism and the Quality of Life, by Alex C. Michalos. 1989. 56 p.

Understanding War, by John McMurtry, with a foreword by Anatol Rapoport. 1989. 68 p.

The Name of the Chamber Was Peace, edited by Janis Alton, Eric Fawcett, and L. Terrell Gardner. 1988. 172 p.